Decreasing Classroom Behavior Problems

Practical Guidelines for Teachers

Decreasing Classroom Behavior Problems

Practical Guidelines for Teachers

John C. Burke, Ph.D.
The Kennedy Krieger Institute and
The Johns Hopkins University
Baltimore, Maryland

SINGULAR PUBLISHING GROUP, INC.
SAN DIEGO, CALIFORNIA

> This book is dedicated to my wife, Carolyn, and to our sons, Joshua and Justin.

```
LB
3011
.B96
1992
```

Published by Singular Publishing Group, Inc.
4284 41st Street
San Diego, California 92105-1197

© 1992 by Singular Publishing Group, Inc.

Typeset in 11/13 Palatino by CFW Graphics
Printed in the United States of America by McNaughton & Gunn

All rights, including that of translation reserved. No part of this publication may be reproduced, stored in a retrieval system, or transmitted in any form or by any means, electronic, mechanical, recording, or otherwise, without the prior written permission of the publisher.

Library of Congress Cataloging-in-Publication Data

Burke, John C. (John Charles)
    Decreasing classroom behavior problems : practical guidelines for teachers / John C. Burke
      p.   cm.
    Includes bibliographical references and index.
    ISBN 1-879105-37-3
    1. Classroom management.   2. School discipline.   3. Behavior modification.   I. Title.
LB3011.B96   1992
371.1'024 — dc20   92-2934
                                                                                           CIP

Contents

Preface v

PART I *INTRODUCTION* 1

1 An Historical Overview 3
2 Understanding Why Children Show Disruptive Classroom Behaviors 7

PART II *PRACTICAL METHODS FOR ASSESSING BEHAVIOR PROBLEMS IN THE CLASSROOM* 15

3 Defining and Counting Behaviors 17
4 Selecting an Assessment Strategy 29

PART III *ESTABLISHING A BEHAVIOR MANAGEMENT PROGRAM* 33

5 Prioritizing Target Behaviors 35
6 Basic Intervention Principles and Procedures 39

PART IV *CONSEQUENCES* 61

7 Positive Reinforcement 63
8 Punishment 79

PART V *METHODS OF INCREASING COOPERATIVE CLASSROOM BEHAVIORS* 85

9 Maximizing Student Cooperation 87
10 Token Economy Programs 95

PART V *(continued)*

11 Teacher-Student Contracts **101**
12 Self-Monitoring Programs **107**
13 Teaching Communication Skills **115**

PART VI *METHODS OF DECREASING DISRUPTIVE CLASSROOM BEHAVIORS* **121**

14 Increasing Other Behaviors That Serve the Same Function **123**
15 Planned Ignoring **127**
16 Time-Out from Positive Reinforcement **131**
17 Response Cost **137**
18 Fixing the Environment **141**

PART VII *ASSESSING THE EFFECTIVENESS OF AN INTERVENTION PROGRAM* **145**

19 Orientation to Program Assessment **147**
20 Program Assessment Strategies **153**

PART VIII *INTEGRATING A BEHAVIOR MANAGEMENT PROGRAM INTO A STUDENT'S INDIVIDUALIZED EDUCATIONAL PROGRAM* **165**

21 Strategies for Designing and Implementing Successful Programs **167**
22 Concluding Comments **181**

References **183**
Glossary **189**
Index **193**

Preface

To become a successful teacher, a person must have training in a variety of areas including instructional methodology, curriculum development, and classroom management; have patience and a true desire to help students learn and develop; and have a great deal of common sense. Without all three, teaching is a frustrating job; with all three, teaching becomes a long-lasting, enjoyable, and successful career. The impetus for writing this book was to add to the training of teachers and instructional assistants by presenting information and practical guidelines that can be used to prevent and reduce disruptive classroom behaviors.

Use of the techniques discussed in this book can enhance learning by students and contribute to a positive classroom atmosphere that can be enjoyed by teachers and students. Although a single book cannot make an individual an expert, the goal of this book is to provide teachers and other school personnel with a working understanding of successful state-of-the-art techniques of classroom management. Based on interdisciplinary research findings reported in the literature and 15 years of practical experience, basic and advanced procedures along with guidelines for their use are presented that can be used to increase student performance and to promote success for teachers and other professionals.

This book is organized into eight sections. Part I provides a brief introduction to classroom management of disruptive behaviors from a teacher's perspective with an emphasis on the development of effective teaching and classroom management strategies. In addition, a framework is presented for understanding why children show disruptive classroom behaviors. Part II provides an overview of practical methods for assessing behavior problems in the classroom. As discussed in this book, great emphasis must be placed on the assessment phase of an intervention program to increase its success. Part III describes the basics of establishing a behavior management program, presenting information on prioritizing and targeting a wide variety of disruptive classroom behaviors. Part IV concentrates on the use of consequences in behavior management.

The next two major sections, Part V and Part VI, present methods designed to alter behavior in a classroom environment. Specifically, Part V provides guidelines on several procedures based on positive reinforcement which can be used to facilitate increases in cooperative and appropriate classroom skills while decreasing disruptive behaviors. Issues and case examples pertaining to these procedures are presented. Part VI presents techniques that can be used to target and reduce inappropriate classroom behaviors, along with issues pertaining to the use of these techniques, and several case examples to enhance the readers' understanding.

Part VII provides information that enables teachers to systematically evaluate the effectiveness of their programs. As is discussed, program evaluation can range from using very simple methods to more involved strategies that some teachers find intriguing. Part VIII focusses on strategies for integrating a behavior management program into a student's Individualized Education Program. In addition, this section discusses methods for facilitating generalization and maintenance of the student's appropriate behaviors.

Acknowledgments

I would like to thank all of the teachers and administrators who have invited me into their classrooms and schools. Through their dedication and efforts, we as a team have been able to help many students. Without entry into their classrooms or, as I call them, their "homes," I would not have been able to produce this book. They have been especially willing to provide feedback regarding my work in the schools and the development of this book. Given their day-to-day work loads, this was not an easy task.

Aside from the professionals, many (too many to name) parents and children have provided me with considerable insight and feedback. My greatest inspiration for writing a book for teachers, instructional assistants, and other school personnel is to disseminate information to promote state-of-the-art educational and behavior management practices for these and other children. We, as professionals, must do everything we can to ensure that children meet success.

The two children who have taught me the most are my own sons, Joshua and Justin. Watching them interact with other children (and adults) has truly allowed me to see children's behavior from a different perspective. My appreciation is also extended to my parents who, throughout my life, have always given me support for my ideas, praise for trying, guidance when needed, and, of course, love. I would also like to thank Ray and Cindy for giving me feedback on the formation of this book; Ray for his insightful comments and Cindy for her feedback as a developing counselor and professional in the field.

In addition, I would also like to thank everyone who has helped me to prepare this book, especially the folks at the Kennedy Krieger Institute and The Johns Hopkins University School of Continuing Studies, Division of Education, and in particular, Alana C. Kane and Sharon McGourty. My thanks are also extended to my friend (and editor) Mike Bender for his advice and patience. Last, I would like to thank my wife, Carolyn. When I am troubled, her positive thinking shines like a beacon for me which allows me to continue with my efforts.

PART I

INTRODUCTION

1

An Historical Overview (From a Teacher's Perspective)

Having students who show disruptive behaviors is not new. Our approach to helping them has changed drastically.

You and a large group of new students are in a room. The goal is to have them learn. Perhaps you are lucky and you have a teaching assistant who will share this adventure. It is likely that some of the children in your class have a history of being disruptive. As you look forward to a wonderful year, you begin to realize that your old textbook on theories of classroom management and last year's two-hour workshop may not be enough to help you deal with situations in which your students are disruptive. In discussing your concerns with other teachers you discover that it is common for teachers to have difficulty translating textbook theories of classroom management into practice. Furthermore, although everyone appreciated the overview of information presented in last year's mini-workshop, it did not provide enough detail to allow participants to gain a working understanding of the principles of effective classroom management.

Although it is not necessary for teachers to know the theories behind classroom management techniques, it is easier to implement them when you have a good understanding of the basic principles. In preparing individuals to become teachers and classroom assistants, it is important to train them in a manner that allows them to generalize their skills to novel problem behaviors and situations. Thus, rather than taking a "cookbook approach" to training professionals in problem behaviors and solutions, this book emphasizes the need for professionals to gain a good working knowledge of the principles that form the basis of the techniques of behavior management while providing numerous applications of the principles through case examples.

Effective teaching involves effective classroom management. Implementing effective classroom management strategies teaches students appropriate and useful skills as well as sets the stage for them to acquire more knowledge in subject areas such as math, English, and social studies. Although some teachers claim they do not believe in using behavior management techniques, all teachers have some classroom rules and a plan to maintain them. Acknowledging the need for training in strategies that facilitate increases in appropriate classroom behaviors and decreases in disruptive behaviors is an important step in becoming a more effective teacher.

While I was being prepared to teach children, the program director, the late Dr. Richard Jamgocian, spoke to a group of us on the importance of having a large repertoire of teaching techniques and drawing on them as needed in different situations. Dr. Jamagocian was right. It is equally important for teachers to have a large array of effective behavior management procedures that can be utilized when necessary and be able to apply them as needed in novel problem situations.

This book is designed to serve as a resource guide for teachers and other classroom personnel. In addition to presenting specific techniques, multiple applications of the principles behind the techniques are included along with case examples based on the author's involvement with teachers. Although volumes could be written on the topic of behavior management, this book concentrates on providing classroom personnel with a good working understanding of some basic principles of behavior management.

The specific principles included in this book are based on systematic investigations conducted by numerous researchers. In addition, and perhaps more importantly, the principles presented in this book were chosen based on my previous experiences working directly with children and while serving as a consultant with teachers and school systems. My work as a consultant has been invaluable in allowing me to gain greater input from teachers, administrators, and parents. By working closely with teachers, I have had the opportunity to formulate, implement, and evaluate many diverse intervention programs. Aside from observing which procedures are effective and which are not, I have been able to receive input from teachers regarding the feasibility of implementing the procedures. While some principles may be quite powerful in producing a change in a student's behavior, teachers must be able to implement the procedures during the course of their daily responsibilities.

2

Understanding Why Children Show Disruptive Classroom Behaviors

Instead of asking why a student is disruptive, it may be more beneficial to ask what function the behavior serves for the student.

Students may show disruptive behaviors for a vast number of reasons and the ways in which professionals try to understand why students show them are equally numerous. Some professionals spend a considerable amount of time attempting to pinpoint an early experience that may have significantly influenced the child. Although early childhood experiences undoubtedly influence later behavior, many students' behaviors worsen while professionals attempt to isolate an original underlying cause.

Other professionals try to determine whether there is an underlying medical basis for the child's behavior problem. Indeed, it is often useful to consult with a physician to rule out an underlying medical basis for a student's disruptive behavior and to determine whether a medical approach is indicated. Typically, however, my medical colleagues have encouraged me to begin a behavioral intervention program as soon as possible.

Although many approaches to understanding students' disruptive behaviors are based on subjective opinion and theory, there is an approach based on systematic research and direct observations of students in classrooms. With its roots in Applied Behavior Analysis (Kazdin, 1978), this approach attempts to determine what function the disruptive behavior serves for the student. Rather than concentrating on determining the original cause of the behavior, it focuses on determining the maintaining cause or the function the behavior serves for the student. In contrast to the difficulty of trying to determine how students originally developed disruptive behaviors, Applied Behavior Analysis helps a teacher determine the reasons why these behaviors continue within a relatively short period of time (Alberto & Troutman, 1990; Cooper, Heron, & Heward, 1987; O'Leary & O'Leary, 1977). As will be discussed in the following chapters, knowing the function the behavior serves leads to the development of an effective intervention program.

ASSESSING THE FUNCTION OF DISRUPTIVE BEHAVIORS

Collecting A-B-C Observations

Referred to as the "ABC" assessment model, this approach involves recording the occurrences of disruptive behaviors exhibited by a student along with some additional information on the situations in which they occur (Bijou, Peterson, & Ault, 1968). In this model, "B" refers to the behavior of concern such as tantrums, dawdling, property destruction, and noncompliance. "A" stands for events that occurred before, or "antecedent" to, the disruptive behavior and may include teacher requests, a sudden change in the topic of discussion, or a change in a daily routine. In a similar manner, the teacher records what occurred following the disruptive behavior. Those events are referred to as consequences (C). Consequences may include a wide variety of events such as "the child did not finish the assignment and went to recess," "the child whined and was given a hug," and "the child was given a lecture on why students should not disrupt the class."

This information can be recorded on any sheet of paper, but many teachers find it easier to use a form such as the one shown in Figure 2-1. At the top of the form, the teacher records relevant information about the child. The remaining space is organized into four columns. The first column includes the date and time

Student's Name_____

Date/Time	Antecedent	Behavior	Consequence

Figure 2-1. *An A–B–C data collection form to record instances of the target behavior displayed by the student. Along with the target behavior, the teacher records the antecedents and the consequences associated with occurrences of the behavior.*

when the child showed the disruptive behavior. The other three columns are used to record the respective antecedents, behaviors, and consequences pertaining to each particular episode. Figure 2-2 is an example of a completed A–B–C data form for a 13-year-old student with mild retardation and a history of striking out at his classmates.

Interpreting The A-B-C Observations

After collecting A-B-C data for a period of time, the next step is to review the data to determine whether there are any clear patterns in the antecedents, behaviors, and consequences. As can be seen in the example in Figure 2-2, the data seem to show that this child typically hit other students after being teased about his poor

Student's Name Mike

Date/Time	Antecedent	Behavior	Consequence
9/17/91 10:20	Mark Teased Mike about his odor.	Mike swung but missed.	Mark left.
9/17/91 1:30	Students were laughing at Mike.	Mike yelled.	They walked away
9/18/91 9:15	Students were holding their noses.	Mike hit one & yelled.	Mike was sent to office.

Figure 2-2. *An example of an A-B-C data form completed for a student who displays aggression.*

hygiene and physical appearance. When I discussed this pattern with the teacher, I was informed that this student rarely showed any concern with his physical appearance and hygiene. As a result of collecting these data, the teacher and I were able to set up a program that targeted these areas. In addition, we also taught him more appropriate strategies to handle situations in which he was teased by other students. Following the implementation of the program, the disruptive behaviors subsided.

Common Reasons Why Students Exhibit Disruptive Behaviors

Although theoreticians could argue for years about why students show disruptive behaviors, the data collected using the A-B-C form provide considerable insight into why a particular student uses disruptive behaviors in terms of the function the behavior may be serving. Presented below are some of the more common functions that disruptive behaviors serve for students.

ATTENTION GETTING. Students of all ages may engage in disruptive behaviors to gain additional attention from their teachers or peers. Most students desire attention and, as a result, have been known to show some very disruptive and hard-to-manage behaviors during class to acquire additional attention. As will be described in Chapter 14, if a student is showing disruptive behaviors to gain attention, there are very direct and successful methods to teach the student that only certain appropriate behaviors gain extra attention. For instance, as shown in Figure 2-3, a student can be taught to raise his hand to get extra attention. Other teachers have taught students to remain "on-task" to get extra attention.

ESCAPING OR AVOIDING SITUATIONS. Some students from a very young age learn that exhibiting disruptive behaviors allows them to escape or avoid certain types of situations (Carr, Newsom, & Binkoff, 1980). Teachers have often reported that students will be disruptive to avoid tests, difficult assignments, or a certain academic topic such as reading or math. For example, Billy, a 10-year-old student with mild retardation, had a history of throwing tantrums. Due to the severity of his tantrums, he was at risk of losing his school placement. Using A-B-C data collection, it was

Figure 2–3. *Teaching a student an appropriate behavior to gain attention, such as raising his hand, often will lead to reduced levels of disruptive behaviors.*

determined that he displayed tantrums only prior to his reading lessons and other situations that involved following written instructions. After formal testing, it was determined that Billy had a very rare vision problem that hindered his efforts in learning to read. His display of disruptive behaviors allowed him to avoid being teased by his peers. As this case illustrates, delineating the function that disruptive behaviors serve may allow school personnel to pinpoint a student's learning disability.

CONTROL. For some students, exhibiting disruptive behaviors may be used to gain greater control over the environment. Control, in itself, is often a reinforcer for such individuals (Koegel, Kern-Koegel, & Schreibman, 1991). For example, a teacher reported that a girl in his class frequently insisted that she wanted to dictate her schedule of activities, and would dawdle and be noncompliant when given requests. Because she would complete other work during these episodes, the teacher concluded that this student was not trying to escape from doing work nor attempting to gain additional attention from the teacher. The A–B–C data clearly suggested that this student was attempting to gain greater control in the classroom. These data led to the development of an intervention program that involved the use of a self-monitoring and a contract system between the teacher and the student. This system gave the student an opportunity to provide some input into her schedule, yet ensured that the teacher was in overall control of the situation.

COMMUNICATION. In the last 10 years there has been increased acknowledgment that some students use disruptive behaviors as a result of having problems communicating their needs, wants, or feelings (Horner & Budd, 1985). This is common for students who have pervasive developmental delays such as some children with autism. Systematic research and informal observations have indicated that tantrums and self-injurious and aggressive behaviors often serve a communicative function for such children (Iwata, Dorsey, Slifer, Bauman, & Richman, 1982). Other children, who are less involved, also use disruptive behaviors as a result of not having sufficient social and pragmatic skills. As will be discussed in Chapter 13 of this book, an approach to help eliminate the disruptive behaviors in these students involves increasing appropriate communication and social skills (Carr & Durand, 1985).

Thus, determining the function that the disruptive behavior serves for a student is one of the first steps in developing an intervention program. Based on research and direct observations, students typically show disruptive behaviors to:

- Gain extra attention.
- Escape or avoid demanding situations.
- Exert control.
- Communicate with others.

After determining the function of the disruptive behavior, the next set of activities involves defining the behavior, and determining the degree to which the student shows the behavior before introducing an intervention. This process will help a teacher to implement an effective intervention program.

PART II

PRACTICAL METHODS FOR ASSESSING BEHAVIOR PROBLEMS IN THE CLASSROOM

Defining and Counting Behavior

Before implementing the program, defining the target behavior is vital as is knowing how often the student shows the behavior.

As a consultant for teachers and schools, I am often asked to participate in advisory meetings involving teachers, psychologists, speech therapists, and administrators.

During the first meeting regarding a student, I often receive a brief report that describes the student. The following is an excerpt from a report that was provided in reference to a 9-year-old boy in a classroom for students with neurological disorders.

> Ralph is a 9-year-old boy with a neurological disorder of unknown basis and with mild retardation. His speech and language is substantially delayed and he is reluctant to interact with other students and adults. He has good fine motor skills, yet has great difficulty with writing. Since the start of the year, he has been very disruptive and requires considerable time from the teacher and assistant.

Having background information on a student is very important and contributes to the process of forming an individualized intervention program. However, it also is necessary, to have a precise definition of the disruptive behaviors being shown by the student. In profiling students with behavior problems, at least equal emphasis should be placed on defining the behaviors of concern in an individualized manner. Along with relevant background information, the definitions of the disruptive behaviors are of great assistance in forming an intervention program.

DEFINING TARGET BEHAVIORS

Precisely defining disruptive behavior involves forming an operational or behavioral definition. A *behavioral definition* is a statement that specifies exactly what behavior is to be observed and targeted in the intervention. A definition should meet three criteria. It should be:

1. objective,
2. clear, and
3. complete.

Objectivity

The definition should refer to observable characteristics of the behavior or environment in which the behavior occurs. Definitions should not refer to inner states or make inferences about the student. Observable characteristics include movement by the student, such as a student running in the classroom or knocking books off a table; making disruptive noise, such as yelling, talking out of turn, or screaming; or inappropriate physical contact with others, such as kicking, hitting, or pushing.

Clarity

The definition should not be ambiguous. After reading the definition, two or more adults should be able to agree that they are observing an occurrence of the target behavior. A typical error in defining behavior is being too vague or general. For instance, to say a student is "aggressive" is too general a definition. Aggressive behavior could be intense hitting for one student, but lightly pushing for a second student, clearly two different behaviors. A good general rule is to provide enough detail to allow two people to agree approximately 80% of the time.

Completeness

Ideally, the definition should delineate the boundaries of the target behavior. Rather than delineating only the target behavior, it is often helpful to indicate what form of the behavior is not included or under what circumstances. For instance, if a teacher defines the disruptive behavior of a student as "He talks too much with other children," it may be wise to indicate that talking to other children is disruptive only during circle time and not during other times, such as recess, when talking with other children is actually encouraged.

Thus, good definitions of target behaviors should be objective, clear, and complete. In addition, the definition should be as brief as possible. Lengthy definitions are often confusing to others and hinder the development of an intervention program. Some examples of definitions of disruptive behaviors and appropriate classroom behaviors that could be targeted for intervention follow.

Sample Definitions

Negative Classroom Behaviors

Aggression
   Billy pushes other students in a rough manner, although he does not hit them with a closed fist.

   Although Mark has never been physically aggressive, he walks up to other students and threatens them by saying such statements as "I'm going to hurt you," and "I'm going to hit you."

Tantrums
   Sally stomps her feet and screams in a loud voice.

   Barbara falls to the floor and becomes very physically agitated while yelling, screaming, and often attempting to hit others.

Noncompliance
   Carol frequently ignores the request and continues with her previous activity.

After being presented with requests, Tom will frequently say, "No, I don't have to do it" and run away from the adult.

Positive Classroom Behaviors

Social Skills
John will go up to other students and initiate an interaction with an appropriate saying such as "How's it going?", "What's going on?", and "Hi guys."

Mary will pause after making a comment or asking a question and allow other students an opportunity to talk.

Remaining on Task
Mark will work for a 15-minute period without interrupting other students.

Sharon will complete an assignment before getting up to play with others.

Getting Help
Devon will raise his hand to get the teacher to provide assistance when needed.

Tarsha will say "excuse me" when she would like to signal the teacher she needs help.

Defining behavior precisely and accurately allows other concerned adults to agree on what behavior should be targeted. In addition, in some instances, this definition can be shared with the student to draw attention to the target behavior. This is especially important when the target behavior is a positive classroom skill.

MEASURING BEHAVIORS

The need to introduce an intervention program is based on the notion that a student does not show certain positive classroom skills and instead is disruptive. The goal of intervention is to eliminate the disruptive behaviors and to ensure that the student learn more productive classroom skills. An intervention program often takes some time to be effective in eliminating the disruptive behavior. As the program is implemented, teachers need to assess the effects of the intervention and to determine whether the student demonstrates a decrease in the disruptive behavior and/or an increase in an appropriate classroom behavior.

Rather than simply judging whether the behavior is present or not present, teachers need to have a system in place to determine the degree to which the student shows the behavior as the program progresses. Using a system helps determine how the student is progressing and gives the teacher information to fine tune the program. After forming a working definition of the disruptive behavior, a teacher can begin to determine the level of the behavior shown by the student.

To determine the degree to which a student shows a disruptive behavior, the teacher needs to use an objective method to record data. Collecting these data also helps the teacher to evaluate the success of a program. It is important to know the level of the disruptive behavior prior to introducing the intervention. The level of the target behavior prior to intervention is referred to as the *baseline*. As a teacher introduces an intervention, the level of the target behavior shown by the student is compared to the level during baseline to assess the effectiveness of the program.

Types Of Assessment Systems

There are three general methods of recording behaviors:

1. Automatic recording
2. Direct measurement of permanent products
3. Observational recording

Automatic Recording

An automatic recording device is an electrical or mechanical apparatus that is activated by the student's responses and makes a record of each response. In many classrooms, teachers use computers to facilitate skill acquisition and to improve on-task performance. Some computer programs have a built-in capacity to record the number of problems completed and the amount of time the student needed to complete the work. This type of a recording is highly precise and requires a low rate of monitoring or direct supervision by the teacher. In addition, this method yields a numerical output, such as number of problems completed, which allows a teacher to chart a student's progress.

Direct Measurement of Permanent Products

Many classroom activities result in products that last long enough to be measured and recorded. For instance, a project completed by a group of students can be used to assess teamwork, if the project is designed to necessitate cooperation to be completed. A student's notes taken during a presentation can be used as a form of outcome measurement. The notes can be reviewed afterwards to determine whether the student was attending to the teacher. A word of caution about using this method: If the teacher does not observe the students during the process, the teacher cannot be 100% assured that the work was completed by the respective student(s).

Observational Recording

Direct observation of students is perhaps the best general approach in documenting the occurrence of target behaviors. Observational recording involves having an observer watch the student while the behavior is being displayed and make a record of the behavior being monitored. There are a few variations of this approach that teachers find useful.

Observational recording is one of the most common general strategies used by teachers to systematically observe student behaviors. This strategy is the most direct method of monitoring changes in a student's behavior. Included in this general strategy are some specific methods to observe and record data on students' behaviors.

FREQUENCY OR EVENT RECORDING. The simplest method to assess the level of the disruptive behavior is to tally each occurrence of the behavior. This approach is referred to as a frequency count or event recording because the teacher records all of the events or occurrences of the behavior. Using this approach a teacher can collect information on the level of a disruptive behavior while

Student's Name_____

	Mon.	Tue.	Wed.	Thu.	Fri.
Week 1					
Week 2					
Week 3					
Week 4					

Figure 3–1. *A sample data sheet to tally each occurrence of a target behavior.*

a student is involved in a lesson. A sample data sheet is presented in Figure 3–1.

In general, the target behavior is recorded if the teacher sees (or hears) the complete behavior. Most often the behavior is of a brief duration and has a definite beginning and end. It is important for the teacher to record all instances of the behavior during a set period of time. Thus, rather than using this method of recording behavior for a student throughout a day, a teacher could record occurrences of the behavior for a specific representative period of time. This sample could then be used to determine the effectiveness of the intervention program.

One advantage of this method is that it is a simple procedure that usually does not interfere with ongoing tasks. Another advantage is that it produces a numerical output that is easy to record. For instance, a teacher can easily tally the number of times a student gets out of his or her seat during a one-hour class or the number of times a student makes disruptive noises during a session.

Teachers also like to use this approach when they need to record more than one behavior for a student. This can be done using a slightly modified version of the data sheet, as shown in Figure 3–2. Teachers have used this method to record successes and accidents while teaching young children proper toileting skills. Specifically, the adult records two discrete behaviors: accidents and successful urinations in the toilet.

In addition, teachers often prefer to use this approach when they need to record behaviors for more than one student. For example, a teacher reported that she frequently used this method to record the number of times several students raised their hands to be called on during a class lesson. These data were used to evaluate the effects of an intervention program designed to increase positive classroom skills and to decrease disruptive behaviors.

Thus, the frequency or tally method of data recording is very useful and can be used by a teacher to observe many different types of disruptive and positive classroom behaviors including those listed below.

Disruptive Behaviors
- Aggression, such as kicking, hitting, or pushing
- Noncompliance to requests
- Verbal disruptive behaviors, such as calling out for a teacher without raising a hand, yelling at another student, or making loud vocal sounds

Positive Classroom Behaviors
- Initiating social interactions
- Raising a hand to be called on
- Following through with a teacher's request
- Following a daily rule, such as getting an activity during free time and sitting down quietly

DURATION RECORDING. Sometimes, it is more important to know how long a behavior lasts than to know how often it occurs. For instance, a student may exhibit one tantrum a day; however, the tantrum may last from a few seconds to a few hours. Duration recording is used if the response varies in duration and it is important to know how long individual episodes last.

In some cases, this approach is implemented in a relatively formal manner, for example, by having a teacher use a stopwatch to record the length of time a student is being disruptive and

Student's Name_____
General Data Sheet
Frequency of Target Behaviors

Date/Time	Behavior 1	Behavior 2	Behavior 3

Figure 3–2. *A sample data sheet designed to record occurrences of three target behaviors for a single student.*

then recording the time on a predesigned data sheet. Other teachers use this approach more informally. For instance, as a student begins to be disruptive, the teacher glances up at the clock on the wall to note the time and again glances at the clock when the student has stopped being disruptive. By recording the starting and ending times, the teacher later can calculate the amount of time the student was disruptive. Again, the teacher would record this information in her log.

This strategy typically is used for several common behaviors including:

Disruptive Behaviors
- Tantrums, which may include either a verbal or a physical component
- Out of seat
- Off-task behaviors, which may include "day dreaming"
- Stereotypies, which are commonly displayed by children with autism and may include hand flapping, rocking back and forth, and twirling objects

Positive Classroom Behaviors
- Time spent completing work
- Social interactions with other students
- Cooperative learning interactions
- Cleaning and organizing the classroom

LATENCY RECORDING. Sometimes, it is important to know how much time elapses before a certain behavior is exhibited. *Response latency* is defined as the amount of time between the end of the request and the beginning of the response. This recording strategy is very useful for teachers who are concerned about students who take too long to follow through with a request or to begin an assignment.

For example, a second grade teacher reported that one of her students frequently dawdled after being given an assignment and never had enough time to complete the assignment. Unfortunately, he was given low grades for not fully completing his work. Rather than targeting "task completion," the teacher felt it was important to teach the student to begin his work in a more expedient manner. She used latency recording to determine exactly how much time expired before the student began his work after being given an assignment. Over the course of three weeks, an intervention program was implemented, and the student showed less and less dawdling. Ultimately, he began his work as quickly as the other students in the class.

Rather than measuring the exact number of occurrences or the amount of time a student displays a target behavior, a teacher often is interested in sampling a student's behavior throughout a day. Although frequency and duration recording may be used, two other methods allow a teacher to get an approximation of the level the student is showing the disruptive behavior: interval recording and time-sampling recording.

INTERVAL RECORDING. Interval recording involves dividing a session into brief equal periods of time. The teacher records the occurrence or nonoccurrence of the behaviors during these intervals. If the target behavior occurs more than once in a given interval, several responses do not need to be scored during that interval. The length of the interval is based on the target behavior, the frequency with which the student displays the behavior, and factors related to the situation, such as how many other students the teacher must be concerned with at the same time. In general, the teacher should use a system that can be easily implemented yet is sensitive to changes in the target behavior whether the student shows increases or decreases. After the teacher collects observations for a period of time, such as one hour, the teacher can compute the percentage of intervals in which the student displayed the behavior. The percentage is an approximation of the amount of time the student was engaged in the target behavior.

For example, Mrs. Dobkin used an interval recording system to gather data on the out-of-seat behavior of a student in her fifth grade class. During two 50-minute periods in the day, one in the morning and one in the afternoon, Mrs. Dobkin used a 5-minute interval system to assess how frequently the student was out of his seat. If the student got out of his seat during the 5 minutes, Mrs. Dobkin placed a "y" on a data sheet that was set up with 10 lines, one for each 5-minute period in the session. At the end of the session, Mrs. Dobkin calculated the percent of 5-minute intervals in which she observed the student out of his seat. If she observed him out of his seat once or twice during a 5-minute period, she counted it as one "yes." This system allowed her to get an index of how frequently the student was out of his seat, rather than an exact amount of time. Although this method did not produce the exact number of times the student was out of his seat, she felt that she had a good system of gathering representative information that allowed her to continue with her lessons.

TIME SAMPLING RECORDING. This method is similar to interval recording except that it does not require continuous observations. A behavior is recorded if part of one or more behavioral episodes is observed to occur within one of a series of *discontinuous* intervals. This procedure gets its name because the observer obtains the measure of the behavior during a sample of the time period rather than during all of it. Teachers have used time sampling to record many ongoing behaviors.

For instance, a teacher might want to get an idea of the degree that a student is working on his assignments during independent seat work. Rather than recording the exact amount of time the student is working on his assignments, she decides to use a time sampling method. Specifically, after giving the student his assignments during the day, she checks on him when the clock is at the one quarter hour mark during those portions of the day the students need to work independently. Thus, on each quarter hour she looks over to the student to observe whether he is actively working on his assignments. Later in the day, she computes the percent of observations she observed him on-task. Although the specific number may vary from day to day, the teacher can compare the data because it is a percentage of observations. The percent represents an index of how much the student was on-task during the day.

4

Selecting An Assessment Strategy

Teachers must select an assessment strategy that allows proper documentation of the target behavior, while permitting the teacher to continue with ongoing activities in the classroom.

FACTORS TO CONSIDER WHEN SELECTING A MEASUREMENT SYSTEM

Selection of the measurement procedure is based on several factors. However, of greatest concern to most teachers are the:

- Target Behavior
- Goal of the Program
- Teacher's Preference

The Target Behavior

The nature of the target behavior helps to determine which recording method should be used. As previously indicated, if the behavior is brief, the teacher can use a relatively simple tally method to record the frequency of occurrence of the target behavior. If the behavior varies in length, the teacher might prefer to record the duration of the behavior.

The Goal of the Program

The goal of the program also helps to delineate which measuring system should be used by the teacher. For example, if the goal of a program is to increase time on task while reducing off-task disruptive behaviors, an interval recording method might be best. This system would allow the teacher to easily record whether the student is on-task or exhibiting disruptive behaviors and provide the teacher with an index of the level of behavior the student is exhibiting. If the goal of a program is to increase the number of times a student displays a behavior, a frequency or tally system might be best.

The Teacher's Preference

The decision regarding which system to use is also based on the teacher's preference and on environmental factors, such as the size of the class and whether there is a teacher's assistant in the classroom. If two systems could be used to record the targeted behavior, for example, a tally method and a time-sampling method, teachers should choose the system that best fits their teaching styles and classrooms. Teachers must feel comfortable in using a system, and the system should not interfere with their other responsibilities.

IMPLEMENTING AN ASSESSMENT STRATEGY

Preparing to Observe Students

Teachers and other school personnel who will be involved in collecting behavioral data should meet prior to observing the student during class. The definition of the target behavior should be reviewed and many examples discussed. In addition, potential problems should be delineated and solutions devised to ensure that the data recording method will provide the needed information.

Problems that arise during behavior observation are sometimes related to observer bias and drift. *Observer bias* is a systematic error in assessment associated with observers' expectancies and prejudices. *Observer drift* occurs when observers' consistency or accuracy decreases for a period of time, such as at the end of a session or day. Besides ensuring that all observers are collecting data in the same reliable manner at the onset of the intervention, it is necessary to check sporadically during the intervention. Determining the degree to which two independent observers agree on their observations is referred to as *reliability* (Hawkins & Fabry, 1979).

General Guidelines Pertaining to Reliability

To facilitate the collection of data in a reliable manner, observers should be given time to acclimate to the setting prior to collecting data. For instance, if an additional person will be coming into the classroom, it is important to find a place for the person in the room so that his or her presence does not interfere with the lesson being taught by the teacher. All observers must record data in exactly the same manner. If the teacher is using a frequency count, the second observer must use the same method. Perhaps most importantly, the adults must come to an agreement on the definition that will be used and have it available for review throughout the program.

The degree of correspondence between two observers, known as reliability, is expressed in numerical terms. To measure reliability, two people observe the same behavior at the same time. For instance, if two observers are going to be recording data on disruptions, they must be present at the same time to see the same occurrences. To calculate reliability, the percentage of agreements between the two observers is calculated. Specifically, the number of times the adults agree (A) is divided by the number of times the adults agree plus disagree (A + D). As illustrated below, this can be written as a formula and expressed as a percentage.

$$\text{Reliability} = \frac{\text{Agreements}}{\text{Agreements} + \text{Disagreements}} \times 100$$

For example, two adult observers have recorded the occurrences of a child's out-of-seat behavior during a 20-minute session using a 30-second interval recording system. For every 30 seconds, the observers recorded whether the student was out of his seat. If the behavior was observed, they recorded a "Y" for yes; if the behavior did not occur, they recorded an "N" for no. The teacher and the second adult observed the student during the same lesson and recorded their observations independently. The results for the first 10 intervals are presented below for both adults.

	1	2	3	4	5	6	7	8	9	10
Teacher	Y	N	Y	Y	N	Y	Y	Y	N	Y
Assistant	Y	N	N	Y	Y	Y	Y	Y	N	Y

In this example, the teacher and the second observer both recorded occurrence of the behavior in the first, fourth, sixth, seventh, eighth, and tenth intervals and nonoccurrence of the behavior during the second and ninth intervals. Thus their observations agree for eight intervals. They disagreed on the third and fifth intervals. To calculate reliability of their observations, the total number of agreements (8) would be divided by the number of agreements plus disagreements (8 + 2) and the result (0.80) would be multiplied by 100. Thus, the reliability would be 80%. Although we try to achieve 90% agreement, 80% is very acceptable. If the agreement is below 80%, the observers should discuss their observations and determine why there are differences. During the discussion, a consensus should be reached that will increase their future agreement scores.

Suppose a teacher and a classroom assistant are attempting to determine the number of times a student hits others in the class, and they want to ensure that their recording is reliable. Rather than using an interval method of data recording, they decide to use a simple tally method in which each occurrence of the aggressive behavior is recorded by placing a mark on a sheet of paper. At the end of the morning, the two adults compare their data to calculate reliability. Rather than using the previously noted formula, they decide to compare their totals. The teacher recorded 14 occurrences of aggression, and the assistant counted 15 occurrences. To calculate reliability, the smaller number (14) is divided by the larger number (15) and the result is multiplied by 100, which yields 93% agreement. This type of reliability is referred to as *marginal agreement*. It is based on the idea that two observers have observed the same specific instances of the target behavior. Although it is easy to calculate, this method inflates reliability estimates.

PART III

ESTABLISHING A BEHAVIOR MANAGEMENT PROGRAM

5

Prioritizing Target Behaviors

> *Going through a sequence of steps helps to ensure that a program has been developed to target the most crucial behaviors.*

Teachers often ask, "What behavior should we work on first?" This question arises because the teacher feels overwhelmed or because the student has many disruptive behaviors and diverse needs. To address this question, it is often helpful for a teacher to go through a series of steps. These steps, along with examples, are presented in this chapter.

STEP ONE: FORMING A LIST OF CONCERNS

The first step in prioritizing the target behaviors is to form a list of the teacher's behavioral concerns related to the student. The list should be fairly complete and should include both disruptive behaviors that need to be decreased and appropriate classroom skills that need to be increased. Teachers often find it useful to ask other individuals to provide input into forming this list.

Mrs. Sloan, a teacher of a student with mild retardation and a severe communication disorder, provided me with the following list of behavioral concerns and asked where to begin. After we reviewed the list, we progressed to the next step in delineating the initial target behaviors.

Inappropriate Behaviors
- Noncooperation
- Tantrums
- Aggression
- Loud vocalizations
- Stereotypies
- Insistence on sameness
- Social withdrawal

Appropriate Behaviors
- Communication skills
- Social skills
- Task completion
- Independent leisure activities
- Self-help behaviors — toileting, dressing, eating

STEP TWO: CHOOSING THE TOP THREE CONCERNS

The number of concerns initially targeted can range from one to several depending on the student and the intervention program, but it often is easier to begin with as few as possible. The exception might be if a teacher is using a token economy system. The exact number must be chosen based on the specific needs of the student and teacher.

Delineating the Disruptive Behaviors

The first concerns which are chosen typically are those that appear to be interrupting the student's education and the class to the greatest degree. A behavior may be deemed very disruptive as a result of several factors including the severity of the behavior, such as loud tantrums; the frequency of the behavior, such as daily arguments with a teacher; and the potential for the behavior to escalate, such as instances of a student being physically agitated and then becoming aggressive.

The top three concerns often include: cooperation, verbal outbursts, and physical agitation. Several behaviors from the original list sometimes can be combined and targeted simultaneously. For instance, verbal outbursts, tantrums, and mild physical agitation are often targeted concurrently, if they all serve the same function (such as attention getting) for the student.

Delineating the Positive Behaviors

Data gathered using the A-B-C data collection method provide a teacher with information on the function that the disruptive behaviors serve for the student. The information gained through this assessment can be used to delineate positive classroom behaviors which can be taught to the student and which can replace disruptive behaviors in the student's repertoire. When choosing positive behaviors to target, it is vital to remember to individualize them and to take into consideration characteristics of the child, such as the student's age, ease in communicating with others, and general level of functioning. In addition, environmental factors, such as the number of other students in the class and the need for a teacher to supervise them as she implements a program for a single student, should be considered.

In the example given earlier, Mrs. Sloan decided that the three top concerns were noncooperation (or, stated more positively, cooperation), communication skills, and social skills. Mrs. Sloan reasoned that, because teaching a student new behaviors requires the student to be cooperative, this behavior should be one of the first to be targeted. In terms of communication skills, she observed that many of the child's tantrums appeared to serve a communicative function. If the student wanted something or wanted to go somewhere, she would often tantrum until she obtained what she wanted. Lastly, appropriate social skills were included in the top three concerns as a result of the A-B-C data collected on the aggression. After analyzing the data, it appeared that the aggression was used to initiate interactions with others. Thus, the teacher chose these initial areas for intervention because she felt they would have the greatest impact on helping the student.

STEP THREE: REVIEWING POTENTIAL TARGET BEHAVIORS WITH OTHERS

The decision to target specific behaviors is based on direct observations of the student and information gathered from other school professionals. Many schools have shifted from self-contained classrooms in which a single teacher is responsible for teaching students to a system in which students interact with a number of different teachers and other professionals across different settings in the school. In these circumstances, it is vital for a teacher to gather information from the other professionals. This information can be used to decide which behaviors are most important to target as well as the best method of intervention. In addition, and perhaps more importantly, reviewing the list of target behaviors with colleagues can help a teacher avoid many unforseen problems.

Aside from discussing the potential target behaviors with other school colleagues, teachers must involve parents. Parents know their children better than anyone. As such, their input is vital and often provides considerable insight into why a student is behaving in a certain manner. Meeting with the parents also ensures that the parents will support the implementation of a particular intervention program. Having support from the home front is not only advantageous from an intervention perspective, but also ensures that the teacher and the parents "speak the same language" and are not at odds with each other. Reviewing the target behaviors with supervisors, colleagues, and parents is mandatory for staff members who are under my supervision.

6

Basic Intervention Principles and Procedures

The procedures we use today are based on principles developed over the past century. Understanding them will serve as the basis for designing tomorrow's programs.

Behavioral intervention programs concentrate on altering the A-B-C patterns that occur in relation to the behavior of concern. Based on decades of research, professionals have formed certain basic principles that serve as the basis of intervention programs used in school settings (Alberto & Troutman, 1990; Becker, Engelmann, & Thomas, 1975a; Birnbrauer, Bijou, Wolf, & Kidder, 1965). Two of the basic procedures pertain to the two general types of variables that are recorded while collecting A-B-C data: the antecedents and the consequences. Given the important role that consequences have in intervention programs, they will be discussed as a separate topic in Part IV.

Four other procedures that have been shown to be invaluable in working with students with diverse problems are also presented in this chapter. The first is referred to as prompting and prompt fading, the second is known as chaining, the third is called shaping, and the fourth is referred to as partial participation.

ANTECEDENTS

Antecedents can include a wide variety of events such as requests or instructions delivered by a teacher; the setting, type of situation, or specific activities such as large group gatherings, the manner in which task materials are presented; a change in a daily routine; the occurrence of loud noises; and the end of recess. Consistent with the need to document whether there is a relationship between the occurrence of the disruptive behavior and certain antecedents, there is an equal need for a teacher to use this information while forming an intervention program. Although there may be many specific antecedents to disruptive behaviors, it generally is useful to group them under three categories:

- Setting variables
- Task variables
- Teacher variables

Setting Variables

Setting variables include the physical arrangement of the environment such as a large unstructured room versus a small well organized study carrel. Also typically included in this category are variables such as class size and the ratio of teachers to students. In addition, setting variables may also include other related factors such as the time of day the activity occurs and the general teaching format that is being used (e.g., small interactive situations between a teacher and students versus a lecture format for presenting new information).

Once the setting variables that are antecedent to the disruptive behavior have been determined, a teacher can use this information while planning an intervention program. For instance, a teacher reported to me that a 10-year-old student in her class was often verbally disruptive during large group activities. Specifically, during the large class activities, this student blurted out answers and became quite upset if the teacher did not call on her. In contrast, during the small group activities, such as the one shown in Figure 6–1, the student appeared to have enough opportunities to provide the answers to the group and would listen

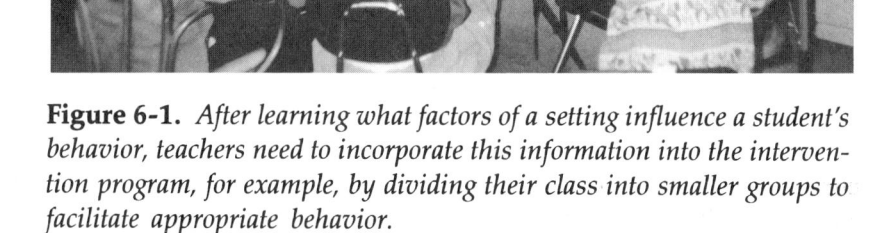

Figure 6-1. *After learning what factors of a setting influence a student's behavior, teachers need to incorporate this information into the intervention program, for example, by dividing their class into smaller groups to facilitate appropriate behavior.*

appropriately while other students contributed. The teacher implemented a program to reduce the disruptions which involved: (a) restating the rule of raising your hand to be called on, (b) providing positive feedback to students who followed through with this appropriate behavior, and (c) calling on the student who had a history of yelling out the answers (if her hand was raised and she was quiet) during the initial portion of many large group activities.

Thus, by determining the setting in which the student was being disruptive, the teacher was able to set up an intervention program that was relatively easy to implement. The information gathered using the A-B-C data collection method provided the basis of forming the intervention program, which was focused on setting the occasion for the student to use an appropriate behavior that served the same function as the disruptive behavior and for the student to be reinforced for her use of the appropriate behavior. Providing the student with opportunities to practice this skill and to receive reinforcement increased the probability that she would use this positive behavior in the future while decreasing the probability that she would use the disruptive behavior. It is important to note that, in such cases, initially it is often necessary to provide the students with many opportunities to use the positive behavior. Over time the teacher can fade the relative number of opportunities to the same number offered to the other students.

Task Variables

In a similar manner, researchers have clearly documented that variables pertaining to the task or subject matter influence a student's display of disruptive behaviors. Task variables include the subject matter (e.g., history, math, or spelling), the method of presenting the task (e.g., lecture, reading, or independent seat work), the degree that tasks are challenging or old, and the degree that tasks are varied during the day or session for students. After the task variables that are antecedent to the disruptive behavior have been determined using the A-B-C data assessment method, an intervention strategy can be devised. Based on systematic research, many task variables are now used to facilitate increased on-task performance and to reduce levels of disruptive behaviors.

Task Variation

A speech therapist reported that an eight-year-old boy with mild retardation and a severe communication disorder had a history of starting each session appearing enthusiastic and on-task, but by the end of the session appeared bored and exhibited high levels of off-task disruptive behaviors. The therapist tried working on different aspects of language from session to session, but this did not alter the boy's pattern of becoming disruptive near the end of each session. The speech therapist and I met to review the data she had gathered from the previous sessions. It appeared that, no matter what the session was focused on, the student became increasingly more disruptive as each session progressed.

Based on the research of Dr. Glen Dunlap and others (Winterling, Dunlap, & O'Neill, 1987), I suggested that the therapist vary the task during each session rather than varying the task only across sessions. This procedure, known as task variation, is a very simple strategy that can be used to increase on-task performance. Teachers who use this procedure typically report that students appear happier, more enthusiastic, and more interested in the activity (Dunlap, 1984). Again, using the A-B-C data collection method led to the development of an intervention program by determining the antecedents to the student's display of the disruptive behaviors.

Shared Control

A second task variable that may influence the child's display of appropriate behavior is referred to as shared control (Koegel, O'Dell, & Koegel, 1987). It has been observed that having students choose topics or activities (usually in the context of a forced choice or multiple choice situation) increases students' enthusiasm for completing the task. For example, as shown in Figure 6-2, having a student choose a topic or a book to write a report on, rather than being assigned a topic or a book, is often implemented in a classroom. Teachers also can incorporate a child's preferred activities or topics while working on less preferred activities.

Teacher Variables

Perhaps the most researched type of antecedent variable that influences student behavior pertains to the techniques and procedures used by teachers and other school personnel. Although numerous teaching strategies have been developed and countless hierarchies of procedures have been described in the literature, a set of basic behavioral teaching principles (procedures) form the basis of many, if not most, instructional interactions between students and teachers. Specifically, these procedures include:

- *Clear instructions or requests,* which are presented to the student by the teacher to initiate a response.
- *Prompts (and prompt fading),* which are used along with an instruction to facilitate a correct response.
- *Chaining,* which involves teaching a complex skill or task by breaking it down into small components and teaching each component to mastery before adding the next component.

Figure 6-2. *Having a student choose from a selection of materials to work on often leads to increased motivation.*

- *Shaping,* which involves reinforcing successive approximations to the ideal response.
- *Consequences,* which involve providing the student with feedback.

Given the important role that consequences play in teaching students, this topic will be discussed as a separate issue in Part IV. Each of the first four procedures is discussed in the following sections and examples of each are provided.

INSTRUCTIONS AND REQUESTS

Teachers report that many disruptive behaviors occur in situations in which an adult presents an instruction or a request to a student. Students may not attend to the teacher while the instruction is being presented and often report that they did not "hear" the instruction. Other students become disruptive following the presentation of an instruction.

As with any procedure, the type of request or instruction used with a student or a group of students must be tailored for the student or group based on several factors including their chronological age and level of functioning. The following are general guidelines pertaining to effective use of instructions and requests.

Keep the Instruction or Request Brief and Clear

For many students, a relatively long, ambiguous instruction increases the likelihood that the child will fail to respond and will exhibit disruptive behavior. This may be the result of frustration or occur simply because the student cannot determine the goal of the task. It is important to remember that a clear instruction for one student may be quite vague for another. A teacher must ensure that an instruction or a request is "understood" by the students. The following are examples of good and poor requests or instructions given to a group of six- to nine-year-old students with mild retardation and behavior disorders.

Examples of Good Instructions

Get your math books out and turn to page 21.

Everyone hang up your coat and then sit down.

Examples of Poor Instructions

Get your math books out after you have put your coats, gloves, and lunches away in your locker and find page 21 and get ready to begin work with sharpened pencils.

Billy, Jan, Mark, uh, uh, class . . . I want all of you to, as quickly as you can, hang up your coats where they belong in your own locker and then take your seats and remain there until I am ready.

The good instructions are concise and clearly stated, whereas the poor instructions are long and contain some irrelevant information. If a student has difficulty responding to complex instructions, the student will find the poor instructions hard to follow. Keeping instructions relatively brief during the initial portion of an intervention program helps guarantee correct responding and may help preclude a student from becoming disruptive to avoid or escape the situation.

Phrase Instructions or Requests in a Direct Manner

Teachers often phrase instructions to children in a question format, for example, "Billy, do you want to come and sit down?" or "Sally, don't you think you should be working?" However, teachers usually do not have any intention of offering the student a choice in such situations. Phrasing instructions or requests in a question format often leads to unnecessary arguments between students and teachers. If the teacher does not intend to offer the student a choice, it is preferable to phrase requests in a nonquestion format, for example, "Billy, please come here and sit down" or "Sally, please finish your work."

Make Sure You Have the Students' Attention Before Presenting Requests or Instructions

Instructions and requests should be presented after you have obtained the students' attention. If a student is not attending to the teacher when the request is being presented, the student may not "hear" the instruction and will be less likely to respond. Ensuring that the student is attending is especially important for children who have difficulty concentrating and focusing their attention. One way to ensure that a student has attended to the presentation of an instruction is to have the student repeat part of the request or instruction. This is especially effective when presenting an instruction to a group of students. For instance, a teacher of a class of 25 second graders used this strategy to ensure that her students would learn to follow requests pertaining to obtaining and returning materials, gathering their lunches and coats, and lining up for recess. After presenting the class with a request, such as "Please get your lunches and line up at the door," the teacher would ask one of the students what they were supposed to do. In this case, the student repeated back "get our lunches and line up." This strategy facilitates cooperation by ensuring that the students are attending to the teacher when the request is presented.

PROMPTS AND PROMPT FADING

Presenting clear instructions and requests to students is important, but a student may need additional assistance. Additional assistance may be needed due to the level of task difficulty, the need to facilitate the student's involvement in an activity, or to ensure that a student complies with a request.

In general, two rules should be kept in mind when using prompts. First, prompts are used to provide additional guidance to a student to ensure that the student performs the desired response. Second, as the student acquires the task or initiates the response in a relatively independent manner, the prompts need to be faded from the situation. Fading of prompts can be accomplished more efficiently if the teacher understands the various types of prompts that can be used and chooses the prompt that is the least intrusive, yet effective.

Types of Prompts

There are three general types of prompts:

- Verbal prompts
- Gestural prompts
- Physical prompts

Verbal prompts include the teacher repeating part of an instruction, for example, "Billy, go get your math book and do page 21 — page 21." Verbal prompts also include saying phrases to a student in a manner to ensure continued performance, for example, "Keep it up," "let's get going," "come on." Verbal prompts also are commonly used when teaching reading. If a child comes across a new word, the teacher can provide the entire word or help the student to sound out the word.

Gestural prompts typically involve some sort of gesture or other motion done with the hand such as waving. This category also includes pointing to the "correct" picture versus the "incorrect" picture. A teacher may use a gestural prompt to help a student locate an object in the classroom by indicating the general area for the student to look in and search for the item. Iconic gestures also are used as prompts. An *iconic gesture* is a gesture that pertains to a concept or idea such as holding your hands far apart in the air to indicate "big" versus positioning your thumb and forefinger in one hand to indicate "little."

Physical prompts are used by a teacher to physically guide the student to respond correctly. When teaching a student to write a letter, teachers sometimes find it useful to guide the student's hand. Physical prompts are used by coaches to help students perform better in sports.

For many young students who need to be taught to comply to requests, teachers often use physical prompts to ensure cooperation. For example, a teacher reported that she had a five-year-old boy who had a history of bolting after she presented the request: "Come here and sit down." Given the potential danger of the child running away, the teacher began a program that initially involved escorting the student to his seat in a firm, yet nonpunishing manner as she presented the instruction. As the student learned not to bolt, the teacher faded the physical prompt first to a gestural prompt, then to a verbal prompt, and eventually removed the prompt entirely.

How to Use Prompts

Learning to use prompts correctly can be achieved by receiving direct feedback from individuals experienced in using prompts. Through sessions, a teacher learns the general manner in which prompts are chosen, implemented, and faded. The guidelines that are given to teachers during training sessions are listed below. Although they are effective, it is advisable to obtain direct feedback prior to, and during, the implementation of prompts.

1. Define the least intrusive, yet effective, prompt

A correct prompt must (a) help facilitate correct responding and (b) be faded over time. The teacher must consider both of these factors when deciding on an initial prompt. Choosing the initial prompt to use with a child typically is based on observing the child and noting the type and degree of difficulty the student is having in performing the targeted behavior or task. In addition, if the target behavior is having the student comply with a request, the teacher needs to delineate the general level of compliance shown by the student. If the teacher typically needs to use gestures with some partial physical guidance, then that level of prompting is best to use initially. It is vital to ensure that the intrusiveness of the physical prompt is minimal. Teachers should not inadvertently teach their students that they must be physically prompted to be cooperative or to respond correctly.

2. After approximately two incorrect (or no) responses, the adult should use the least intrusive prompt to guide the targeted response

Prompts should be used only after it has become clear that they are needed. Therefore, teachers need to allow a student to attempt to respond without prompts. Again, if the target behavior is compliance, the teacher's common sense should be used to decide whether a prompt is necessary to ensure the safety of the student and others during the initial portion of a program.

3. After obtaining a desired level of responding, the teacher should begin to reduce the level of intrusiveness of the prompt

Because the prompt must be faded from the situation, the teacher should begin to reduce the intrusiveness of the prompt as soon as the student begins to perform the targeted response in a more fluent manner. Reducing the intrusiveness of a prompt is not a science. The teacher must pay close attention to the student's rate of acquisition and mastery of the new skill. In addition, although physical prompts are very effective in ensuring that a student follows through with a request, they are difficult to fade. Therefore, the use of full physical prompts should be restricted to situations that clearly necessitate their use.

Fading the Prompt

Although the intrusiveness of each prompt is relative to the preceding prompt, typically, the hierarchy of most to least intrusive prompts is:

Full physical prompt
Partial physical prompt
Gestural Prompt
Verbal prompt

If a therapist has difficulty fading a prompt, it may be necessary to use smaller steps in reducing the intrusiveness of the prompt. Often it is necessary to try several different prompting strategies.

Examples of Possible Prompting Strategies

For a given target behavior, a teacher could use a multitude of different prompts. Listed below are some examples of prompts that have been used by teachers.

Target Behavior: Increasing Appropriate Initiation Skills

The teacher of a group of preschool children reported that a student had a history of hitting, kicking, and pushing others. Based on A-B-C data, it appeared that the student used these behaviors as a method of starting social interactions with other children in the class. Instead of using a punishment-based program, the teacher wanted to use a program that involved increasing other behaviors that served the same function. To increase the student's use of appropriate greeting skills, the teacher modeled and prompted the skills. The following prompting hierarchy was delineated:

Full Physical Prompt
Walking the student over to another student, modeling a verbal greeting and encouraging the student to initiate and play with the other child.
Partial Physical Prompt
Starting the student to go over in the direction of another child and encouraging the student to initiate and play with the other child.
Gestural Prompt
Pointing or motioning with a hand for the student to go towards the other child and encouraging the student to initiate and play with the other child.
Verbal Prompt
Repeating the relevant portion of the instruction (e.g., "Go say 'Hi' and play with Bob — go say 'Hi' ").

Target Behavior: Eating a Meal Using a Fork

It is common for teachers of students with disabilities to report that they have trouble teaching their students to eat independently with a fork or spoon. As part of an intervention program, I often suggest the use of prompting and prompt fading. Some examples of prompts that vary in terms of their intrusiveness and that teachers have found useful while working on this target behavior follow.

Full Physical Prompt
   Placing the child's hand on the fork and holding the child's hand and the fork as a bite of food is taken.
Partial Physical Prompt
   Placing the child's hand on the fork and *partially* guiding the fork up to the mouth.
Gestural Prompt
   Pointing toward the fork and modeling the proper use of the fork.
Verbal Prompt
   Repeating the relevant aspect of the instruction (e.g., "Use your fork — the fork").

Target Behavior: Cooperation

As children grow up, they are faced with the necessity of learning that certain "rules" exist and that they need to cooperate with teachers. Elementary school teachers frequently report that they have a student who responds in a cooperative manner only to a very small number of requests presented during the day. Often, we set up a program that involves increasing cooperation across many different situations and tasks. In the beginning of this program we typically pick a task that is not too difficult and which we can prompt the child to complete. For example, the task might involve teaching the student to sit in a chair on request. The following is a prompting hierarchy that has been shown to be effective with numerous children.

Full Physical Prompt
   Gently holding a child by the hands or shoulders and escorting him to the chair as the instruction "Go sit down" is being given.
Partial Physical Prompt
   Turning the child to the chair while presenting the instruction.
Gestural Prompt
   Pointing or motioning with a hand toward the chair while presenting the instruction.

Verbal Prompt
Repeating the relevant aspect of the instruction, such as "Sit down in the chair — sit down."

Designing Prompts

Although I cannot provide you with direct feedback on your performance in developing effective prompts via this book, it is important to practice developing prompting hierarchies and to discuss them with other colleagues, especially with individuals who have received direct training in this area. Some target behaviors for which teachers frequently request assistance in developing an effective intervention are listed below. Try to design some prompting hierarchies for each.

Target Behavior: Learning to Color in the Lines

Full Physical Prompt
_____
_____
_____

Partial Physical Prompt
_____
_____
_____

Gestural Prompt
_____
_____
_____

Verbal Prompt
_____
_____
_____

Target Behavior: Swinging a Baseball Bat

Full Physical Prompt
_____
_____
_____

Partial Physical Prompt

Gestural Prompt

Verbal Prompt

Target Behavior: Learning to Use a Tape Recorder

Full Physical Prompt

Partial Physical Prompt

Gestural Prompt

Verbal Prompt

Target Behavior: Writing Letters and Words

Full Physical Prompt

Partial Physical Prompt

Gestural Prompt

_____
_____
_____

Verbal Prompt

_____
_____
_____

CHAINING

Chaining is defined as teaching a complex skill or task by breaking it down into small parts or components and teaching each subcomponent to mastery before adding the next component. Chaining is very useful, whether you are a teacher of students with or without disabilities or of students in primary or high schools (Bellamy, Horner, & Inman, 1979). Teachers commonly are faced with the need to teach very complicated tasks to students. Understanding the principle of chaining can help teachers to enable the students to meet success, while reducing the likelihood that they will exhibit disruptive behaviors to avoid the task.

Teachers frequently use this principle when they divide a large content unit into subsections and lessons and teach the students to master the particulars of each lesson before moving to the next lesson. Math teachers use chaining when they teach their students long division. They break the task of long division into several steps and have the students complete each step correctly before moving on to the next step. Ultimately, the students are presented with long-division problems which they are able to complete independently.

Speech therapists use chaining when they are teaching a student with articulation errors to pronounce a sound correctly in the context of a word. First, the student is required to produce the sound in isolation. After the student masters pronouncing the sound correctly in isolation, the student is required to produce the sound in syllables. Subsequently, the student will learn to produce the sound in the context of words and then while speaking in sentences.

Teachers in special education use chaining with students while teaching a wide variety of skills and behaviors. For instance, a complex task such as shoe tying can be broken down into components and taught individually to a student. Many teachers teach a child how to tie a shoe by breaking down this task into eight steps. Using this approach, the teacher teaches a student the first step until the student can perform it reliably. Subsequently, each additional step is taught to a mastery level. If a teacher teaches the first step and then moves through the steps in order, this would be called *forward chaining* (Wilson, Reid, Phillips, & Burgio, 1984). If a teacher has the student learn the last step first, it would be referred to as *backward chaining*. After the student masters the last step, the teacher has the student perform the second-to-last step and then the last step. This process continues until the student can successfully complete all steps (Bellamy, Horner, & Inman, 1979).

The principle of chaining also can be used to teach a student to complete long and seemingly laborious tasks. For example, a teacher reported that she had a 10-year-old student who had severe difficulties completing assignments. Specifically, after being given a page of work, she typically completed only one fourth to one third of it before acting disruptive. Her disruptive behaviors included severe tantrums, aggression, and "emotional outbursts." Although the student "knew" the material, the teacher reported that the student could not work for long periods of time.

Based on information obtained from the teacher and the parents, a program was devised that emphasized teaching the student to complete increasing amounts of work prior to being allowed to take a break. Because she had considerable success completing one fourth of her work, the program initially involved having the teacher give the student approximately that portion. After meeting success, the teacher permitted the student to take a brief break. As the student met success consistently, the amount of work was slowly increased by adding additional problems. On successful completion of the increased work, the student was given slightly longer breaks. This process continued until she consistently completed her entire assignment.

Correctly using the principle of chaining facilitates success for a student by simplifying the difficulty of the task (or subtask) that is presented to the student at any particular time. By meeting more success, the student will be less likely to want to escape or avoid the task by exhibiting disruptive behaviors. Teachers can easily incorporate this principle while working on academic, social, leisure, and daily living skills. After learning to correctly use this principle, teachers have often commented that they are very surprised by how quickly their students can learn very difficult and advanced tasks.

SHAPING: REINFORCING APPROXIMATIONS OF THE IDEAL RESPONSE

From a traditional perspective, shaping involves reinforcing closer and closer approximations of the ideal target response (Becker, Engelmann, & Thomas, 1975b). Shaping is commonly used by teachers to increase the verbal repertoires of students. For instance, a teacher reported that a young boy with severe retardation had great difficulty learning to correctly say new vocabulary words such as drink, cup, food, and names of toys. Rather than providing reinforcement only for the ideal target response, the teacher reinforced the student's approximations (e.g., "cu") for the target word (e.g., "cup"). Over subsequent sessions, the teacher reinforced only closer and closer approximations of the target word.

Shaping also is commonly used by teachers who are teaching students penmanship. Initially, when children are required to write their names, the alphabet, or numbers, the legibility of their work is not always up to "standards." However, rather than demanding that they initially write each letter or number perfectly, teachers will reward the students for improving over time by reinforcing better and better approximations of the letters, numbers, and words. Physical education instructors often use this principle while teaching their students to perform complicated activities or movements such as swinging a golf club. Music teachers incorporate this principle while teaching their students to perform musical compositions.

Teachers of older students with disabilities frequently use this principle while targeting numerous complex behaviors such as vocational work skills. For instance, a teacher of a 19-year-old student with moderate retardation was given the task of teaching the student to serve as an assistant to a landscaper. As part of his job responsibilities, the student had to learn to rake up leaves. Instead of reinforcing the student only for a perfect job, the teacher initially reinforced the student for a good approximation. During subsequent sessions, the teacher reinforced the student for a more thorough completion of raking up the leaves. Ultimately, the student was able to rake up leaves very efficiently and neatly.

Although using shaping as a separate procedure is useful, teachers find it helpful to combine the use of this principle with the principle of chaining to further facilitate a student's success in mastering new and difficult tasks. Both procedures help students acquire very complex tasks in a more efficient manner. Students can meet with much more success when teachers systematically use these principles.

PARTIAL PARTICIPATION

In recent years the concept of partial participation has emerged. Simply stated, *partial participation* refers to the idea of having a student be partially involved in activities, tasks, or situations. The emphasis is on:

- Providing the student with many and diverse opportunities to use a skill across situations.
- Involving the student in a manner that virtually guarantees the student success.
- Reinforcing the student for being involved.
- Increasing the degree of a student's involvement in the task over time.

Teachers use the principle of partial participation while working with diverse behaviors across structured and social situations. For example, Mr. Thomas, a teacher of seriously emotionally disturbed children, used this principle to increase his students' involvement in group activities. The students in his class had a history of failing to work cooperatively with others. Mr. Thomas initially set up activities that required only minimal participation by the students. After the students started to demonstrate success working with each other, Mr. Thomas slowly increased their involvement while fading himself from the activities.

The principle of partial participation also can be used to increase cooperation with teachers. A teacher might take advantage of commonly occurring situations that involve the students' cooperation. As the student cooperates, the teacher helps the student by facilitating successful task completion, as shown in Figure 6–3. Following the student's cooperative efforts, the teacher provides positive social attention along with any naturally occurring reinforcement that results from the completion of the activity. For

Figure 6–3. *Using the principle of partial participation, a teacher can ensure that a student completes a task correctly and experiences success.*

students who typically fail to be cooperative, the first situations and tasks chosen should be those preferred by the student. For example, Jane was a 7th grade student with moderate retardation and a history of tantrumming several times a day when presented with common requests such as "get your books," "put your sweater away," and "sit at your desk." Her tantrums consisted of yelling profanity, falling to the floor, knocking over books, waving her hands in the air, and on some occasions hitting the teacher with a fist. The intervention program initially involved having the teacher set up preferred activities and tasks for Jane's involvement. Aside from using tasks that were highly motivating for Jane, the teacher initially provided Jane with positive social praise for any attempt to comply. As Jane began to exhibit compliance consistently, the teacher began to encourage Jane to accomplish more in an independent manner. As Jane became very cooperative with all of the activities she preferred, the teacher began to intersperse less preferred tasks during the day. Although not always fully correct in her responses, Jane began to show increased cooperation in most of the day-to-day requests presented by the teacher. As with any procedure, partial participtation must be individualized for the student.

The principle of partial participation also incorporates effective prompting. Research conducted by Dr. Robert L. Koegel and his colleagues (Koegel & Egel, 1979) suggests that prompting a student to meet success for a period of time will facilitate more attempts. If the student attempts to respond more frequently, it follows that the student will obtain success more frequently (Churchill, 1971; MacMillan, 1971). With increased success, the student receives more reinforcement which further contributes to increasing positive behavior and lessening disruptive behaviors.

When the principle of partial participation is presented to a group of teachers, there are some common reactions. Some teachers remark that the idea seems too simple to have such a powerful effect. My reply usually begins with: "No one said that behavior management has to be complex." Furthermore, from my perspective, the simpler the program, the better — and the more likely it will be used.

Indeed, teachers usually begin to use this principle in their classrooms very soon after being trained in it. Teachers modify activities for their students in a manner that increases success for the students. By increasing the likelihood for a student to be successful, a teacher also ensures success for the teaching staff. Because many disruptive behaviors are used by students to avoid hard, difficult, or new tasks, this principle has the potential to substantially reduce the likelihood of students exhibiting disruptive behaviors. Although simple, this principle is one of the most powerful procedures a teacher can use to reduce classroom behavior problems.

PART IV

CONSEQUENCES

7

Positive Reinforcement

> *One of the most efficient strategies for altering behaviors is to alter the consequences that follow them.*

Consequences are events that follow the behavior or come after the behavior of concern. Based on Applied Behavior Analysis research, consequences that are functional reinforcers (or punishers) can substantially influence behavior. When collecting A-B-C data, the teacher documents the consequences that naturally followed the behavior of concern and might have influenced the students display of the particular behavior. These consequences may include escaping from a demand, receiving additional attention from a teacher or from other students, obtaining a preferred object, or participating in a fun activity. From an intervention perspective, arranging effective consequences is the most important aspect of any program. An overview of the principles of using effective consequences based on positive reinforcement is presented in this chapter.

THE PRINCIPLE OF POSITIVE REINFORCEMENT

Reinforcement refers to the procedure used to increase the probability (or rate) of a behavior by arranging for a reinforcer to follow the behavior in a contingent manner (Catania, 1984). Virtually any event, object, or social activity that is preferred by the student may be used as a reinforcer. However, technically a *reinforcer* is defined as any "stimulus" that follows the occurrence of a behavior, and increases the probability (or rate) of that behavior. The most important rule of reinforcement is the idea that a reinforcer is only a reinforcer if the child finds it reinforcing. It must lead to an increase in the target behavior before it can be called a true reinforcer. Before it has been shown to be a reinforcer, it typically is referred to as a potential reinforcer.

Given the importance of reinforcement, considerable research has been conducted to refine its use in educational and other settings (Hall & Hall, 1980). As discussed in the next section, there are categories of reinforcers. An understanding of these categories helps teachers to design effective intervention programs.

TYPES OF REINFORCERS

Primary Reinforcers

Primary reinforcers are stimuli that have a biological importance to an individual. Historically, the most commonly employed primary reinforcers are edible reinforcers such as raisins, nuts, cookies, candies, or drinks. Again, the specific item that can effectively serve as a primary reinforcer depends on the preferences of the student. Some students like fruit juice, others may prefer water. In general, teachers use primary reinforcers when it is very important to have a powerful reinforcer to facilitate quick changes in a student's behavior and when other secondary reinforcers have failed to work.

Although edibles and drinks typically promote rapid increases in appropriate behavior, many teachers and other professionals have noted that it is difficult to fade these reinforcers from their programs. If food reinforcers are used with students to facilitate acquisition of behaviors, the teacher must have a plan to fade them from the program. Unfortunately, this is not always an easy task. Some students become "hooked" on the primary reinforcers and learn to work only for such items.

A second type of primary reinforcer is referred to as a *sensory reinforcer.* These include a wide variety of events that are perceived by the child through the senses and the student finds enjoyable (Dewson & Whiteley, 1987; Fehr, Wacker, Trezise, Lennon, & Meyerson, 1979). Auditory sensory reinforcers include music, certain noises, or speech. Visual sensory reinforcers include watching a colorful display or the movement of objects such as pinwheels. Tactile reinforcement includes patting the student on the back or on the arms, or giving a student a hug. Kinesthetic sensory reinforcers include swinging, sliding down a slide, and riding a scooter. Such reinforcers are often preferred by teachers who need a powerful reinforcer for a student but would like to avoid edibles.

Secondary Reinforcers

Secondary reinforcers are items or events that have become reinforcers for a student. Included in this category are items such as toys, balloons, and happy faces (Dunlap, Koegel, Johnson, & O'Neill, 1987). As shown in Figure 7–1, stickers are often used as an effective reinforcer. A wide variety of events and activities have been used as secondary reinforcers (e.g., watching a favorite movie, playing in a park, attending a sporting event, having more time to use a computer in the classroom, and being line leader). As with any reinforcer, the student must view the item or event as being reinforcing for it to serve as a true reinforcer. Secondary reinforcers form the basis of many intervention programs, such as point systems, student-teacher contracts, and token economies. The use of these reinforcers is discussed in Chapters 9, 10, and 11.

Natural and Direct Reinforcers

Natural and *direct reinforcers* are reinforcers that are directly related to the task or activity the student is working on (Bloom & Lahey, 1978). For example, a class of sixth grade students is given an assignment to write a report on tide pools. Following the completion of their reports on Friday, they will be allowed to attend a special trip to the beach to visit the tide pools. Some students who typically fail to complete a report on time for just a good grade are more motivated to complete the report on time if a special consequence is in place. During the early part of the school year, a

Figure 7-1. *Teachers commonly use stickers as reinforcers for students who complete a difficult assignment.*

teacher friend of mine implements this type of contingency. In addition, she prompts or guides the students through the completion of their first report to ensure that they all work earnestly on their reports and meet success. She feels very strongly that prompting the students to success and having the special consequence in place early in the year motivates the students in her class to complete the next report.

Teachers and speech therapists often use direct or natural reinforcers while working with students who are learning to communicate more effectively. For example, a teacher who is attempting to increase a student's initial lexicon will often use toys or other items that the student finds reinforcing. As the student is learning to verbally communicate to obtain items, the teacher will provide the item to the child rather than giving the child a general reinforcer that has little, if anything, to do with the word. For instance, one young boy said "ba" for *ball* and was allowed to play with the ball for a brief period of time. Many years ago, some professionals would have provided the child with a piece of candy or just with social praise such as "good talking." Using direct or natural reinforcers has been shown to help such students learn effective communication skills (Koegel, O'Dell, & Koegel, 1987).

Thus, in general, direct and natural consequences are reinforcers that are either part of the activity or have a functional relationship with the response. These reinforcers motivate a student to remain on task while reducing the likelihood that the student will exhibit disruptive behaviors to escape or avoid demands, requests, and previously difficult learning situations. It behooves a teacher to plan activities in a manner that leads to students receiving a natural or direct reinforcer as a consequence for demonstrating positive classroom behavior.

Generalized Conditioned Reinforcers

When a reinforcer is associated with a variety of behaviors or with access to a variety of other primary or secondary reinforcers, it is referred to as a *generalized conditioned reinforcer*. The most common generalized conditioned reinforcer is money. Older students can earn money for performing a wide variety of jobs and then spend the money for numerous back-up reinforcers. Rather than money, however, many teachers use tokens. Providing tokens to students contingent on their display of appropriate behaviors is a common method of implementing a behavior management program for an entire class. Because each student can use the tokens to "purchase" his or her choice of preferred back-up reinforcers, this type of reinforcement program is useful for an entire class.

DELIVERING POSITIVE REINFORCERS

As with any procedure, a few guidelines must be followed to ensure that success is achieved.

The Reinforcer Should Be Reinforcing to the Student

This may seem obvious, yet many professionals choose reinforcers based on their past experiences with other students. For instance, one teacher voiced dismay that her program was not working with a first-grade student named Ralph: "Other students like stickers, why doesn't Ralph like them? Reinforcement must not work with Ralph!" Her next step was to use a program based on punishment.

Reinforcers must be chosen on an individualized basis. Many students do not particularly like and will not work for stickers. This does not mean that a program based on reinforcement will not work. It means that stickers do not serve as reinforcers for every student and that teachers need to delineate other items that can serve as reinforcers. In Ralph's case, the teacher was advised by a colleague that hand-drawn stars served as powerful reinforcers for completing assignments. Prior to implementing a punishment-based program, the teacher implemented the suggestion as shown in Figure 7-2. Ralph showed increases in positive classroom behaviors and reductions in disruptive behaviors.

Figure 7-2. *Although some students like stickers, others prefer hand-drawn stars or some other variation.*

Reinforcers Must Be Preferred by the Student

If a student has little, or no, interest in obtaining an item or participating in an activity, it will not serve as a reinforcer. A student must want the item or desire to participate in the activity. The more the student wants the item, or to participate in the activity, the more likely it is that these items or events will serve as reinforcers. Ultimately, the reinforcing value of an item or an activity must be demonstrated by an increase in the target behavior. Although other aspects of an intervention program can affect how successful the program is, failing to find a powerful reinforcer has the most dramatic effect on the outcome.

Reinforcers Must Be Checked During the Program

Because an object or activity is preferred one day, and serves as an effective reinforcer, does not necessarily mean the same item will serve as a reinforcer throughout the intervention program. The degree that something is "liked" and serves as a reinforcer may change from day to day for a number of reasons.

- A student may lose interest or get tired of participating in an activity.
- If a teacher is using edibles, it is very common for students to become "full."
- A student may find something else that he or she prefers.
- It is common for today's popular small toys to become yesterday's "junk."

The central point is that a teacher cannot assume that an item or activity that serves as a reinforcer one day will remain a reinforcer over time. The strength of reinforcers must be re-evaluated over time and, if necessary, other items or activities must be incorporated.

Social Reinforcers Should Not Be Ambiguous

If a teacher is using social attention as a reinforcer, the type of attention should not be ambiguous. Saying "Great job" with a frown sends a mixed message. Saying "Good job, for you, Barbara," in a dull voice may actually serve as a punisher for Barbara who is truly trying very hard with a difficult task and feels that her efforts are just as good as anyone else's in the class.

As shown in Figure 7-3, the teacher's message should be very clear. This is especially true when using social praise with students who actually need a tangible reinforcer. For such students, social praise often is combined with tangible reinforcers during the initial portion of intervention programs. However, because social attention is "free" and often highly desired by students, teachers should attempt to use positive social attention frequently as a consequence for appropriate behavior. Especially in the beginning of an intervention, the teacher should provide positive social attention frequently to a student when the student shows appropriate and productive classroom behaviors. As the student continues to make progress, the frequency and amount of social attention can be faded slowly to a more naturally occurring

Figure 7-3. *If a teacher uses social praise as a reinforcer, the message of doing a great job should be very clear.*

level. This method must be individualized and is based on the idea that social attention has been shown to be a reinforcer for the particular student.

Reinforcers Should Be Given to the Student Immediately

In many, if not most, cases teachers need to deliver a reinforcer to a student immediately following the student's demonstration of the positive behavior. This is especially important during the initial portion of an intervention program. Delivering the reinforcer immediately after the student shows the positive classroom behavior helps a student to see the connection between the appropriate behavior and the positive consequence. Even older students and adults like to receive reinforcers soon after performing a difficult or challenging task. After a student has clearly shown improvement, delivery of the reinforcer may be modified to occur after an increased period of time or after a greater number of positive behaviors has been demonstrated by the student. This issue will be discussed in light of the interventions presented in Part V.

Reinforcers Should Be Contingent

Although a teacher may feel sorry for a student, providing the student with a reinforcer when it is not deserved can be more harmful than helpful (Koegel, Russo, & Rincover, 1977). This is called providing noncontingent reinforcement, and it sends the student a mixed message. It may tell the student that he can get away with not trying his best, or even worse, it may tell the student that the teacher is not serious about upholding the classroom rules. Once rules have been set, the teacher needs to uphold them consistently. How consistently? The more consistently a program is implemented, the more likely it is that the intervention will be successful. If a program is inconsistently implemented, the program has a very small chance of working. Once a rule is in place, use common sense and stick to it.

Consistent implementation of a reinforcement program should also occur across different adults and situations. Although this is true for most, if not all, students, consistency is vital when working with children who fail to generalize treatment gains across settings. In fact, limited generalization may be due to inconsistencies in the way adults intervene with a student. When a teacher is forming an intervention program for a student, all concerned adults should become involved, at least to the extent of being informed that a special program is being planned. Involving others across situations in the formation and implementation of a treatment program promotes success and avoids unnecessary problems.

FADING TO NATURALLY OCCURRING REINFORCERS

During the implementation of an intervention program, teachers often provide students with reinforcers that otherwise are not available to them. For instance, teachers who work with students with severe and profound retardation and severely disruptive behaviors often use primary reinforcers in the form of food and drink to produce an initial change in the target behavior. However, after the program begins to work, professionals need to reduce their use of these primary reinforcers and gradually shift to the use of naturally occurring reinforcers such as social praise (Stokes & Baer, 1977). The teacher must make a gradual change from using food and social praise to the use of social praise only. This gradual shift can be initiated by reinforcing every second response with both a primary reinforcer and social praise and the first response with social praise only. If this does not produce significant change in the student's display of the target behavior, the teacher can continue to further fade the use of the primary reinforcer in a gradual manner.

Teachers who work with students in vocational settings commonly report a need to fade their use of one reinforcer to a reinforcer that occurs naturally in the workplace. For example, a 19-year-old student with mild-to-moderate retardation initially needed to be given social praise by his vocational teacher for remaining on task. As the program continued, the vocational trainer began to fade his use of social praise while one of the store's assistant managers began to provide the individual with an occasional comment like "Looks good" or "Keep up the good work."

If, in either of these cases, the teachers had not used the initial reinforcers, the programs might not have been successful.

However, on the other hand, if their use had not been faded, problems pertaining to generalization and maintenance of the student's gains might have occurred. There is a major advantage of using a functional/direct reinforcer during the initial portion of an intervention program. Using natural and direct reinforcers initially will help promote generalization and maintenance of the treatment gains from the beginning of the program.

CHOOSING REINFORCERS

Professionals have begun to specify procedures or methods to help teachers delineate functional reinforcers (Green, Reid, White, Halford, Brittain, & Gardner, 1988; Hall & Hall, 1980; Pace, Ivancic, Edwards, Iwata, & Page, 1985). In general, these methods can be divided into informal and formal selection strategies. Regardless of which system is used, the goal is to delineate potential reinforcers prior to using them in an intervention program.

Informal Selection Methods

Teachers often use a very easy method to delineate potential reinforcers for students. Teachers observe the students during free time and note what they like to do. Subsequently, teachers use these activities or items as potential reinforcers. Other teachers simply ask students to provide a list of preferred items that may serve as reinforcers. For students who can communicate effectively, gathering a list of potential reinforcers is very useful. Of course, the reinforcers must be plausible. If a student says he would like to get a car for being good in class, some negotiating is in order.

Sometimes teachers use a "reinforcer store," which contains a wide variety of reinforcers, as shown in Figure 7–4. The store is often used in conjunction with a token program, a point system, or a student-teacher contract system. Prior to the initiation of an intervention program, the teacher and student decide which item or special activity the student will be working to receive as a reinforcer. This system provides the student with a tangible goal, which is a constant reminder for the student. Although tangible reinforcers are useful in motivating a student during the initial portion of an intervention program, such reinforcers need to be faded as the student makes consistent progress.

Figure 7-4. *A student is allowed to trade his tokens for a valued item in a reinforcer store.*

Formal Sampling Procedures

For some students, teachers have reported that it is difficult to determine items or activities that will serve as effective reinforcers. Delineating preferred activities and items to serve as reinforcers is especially important for students who are not motivated by social attention. Various methods to delineate potential reinforcers have been described in the literature (Hall & Hall, 1980).

The following guidelines are offered to help a teacher be more assured that items or activities will serve as reinforcers.

1. Form a list of items and activities that may serve as reinforcers. This list should be based on direct observations of children while playing, eating, or involved in other settings. In addition, information reported by other adults can be included.
2. Present these items to the student in pairs and note which item the student prefers.

3. When the item is removed, note whether the student attempts to regain the item.
4. Present the top five or six most preferred items in pairs and note which item is desired. Repeat this procedure for several combinations of the items.
5. Tabulate the number of times the student preferred each item.
6. Organize the list of items from the most preferred to the least preferred.
7. The most preferred items should be used first as the reinforcers while working with the student on new or challenging tasks.
8. This process should be conducted as frequently as the data suggest.

Using a formal method to assess which items are most preferred by a student does not guarantee that those items will be effective in serving as reinforcers throughout an intervention program. However, this process does give teachers a starting point and helps to ensure that an item is indeed a reinforcer before the start of the program. The only true method of determining that an item does serve as a reinforcer is to show that providing the student with the item or activity contingent on the student displaying the target behavior increases the particular behavior.

WHY DOES A REINFORCER WORK?

A reinforcer increases a behavior, because the individual is willing to work to obtain the item. If the student does not want the item, the item will not serve as an effective reinforcer. A student may not want the item or not be willing to work for the item for a number of reasons.

A student may already have free access to the item.
If an item is freely available to a student, using the item in a program that requires the student to work for it probably will not produce any change in the student's behavior. Only "special items" that a student does not have free access to should be used as part of the intervention program. Restricting the student's access to an item that was previously accessible may result in addi-

tional disruptive behavior. Avoid additional problems by picking different items or by restricting access to previously accessible items through a response-cost program, as described in Chapter 17.

A student may be tired of a particular item or activity.
After a particular item has been used as a reinforcer for a period of time, students often lose the desire to obtain it. This is true whether the item is a game, the opportunity to play with a toy, or the student's favorite food or drink. When a student is tired or full of a particular item, this condition is referred to as a state of *satiation*. Satiation is the opposite of *deprivation*, which is a condition that must be met if reinforcers are to be optimally effective. If a student has been without a particular favorite item for a period of time, it is more likely that the item will serve as a strong reinforcer.

HOW FREQUENTLY SHOULD STUDENTS BE REINFORCED?

How often a student needs to be reinforced depends on several factors. One is the history of the student's exhibition of the target behavior. For instance, if the target behavior is cooperation and the student has rarely been cooperative in the past, the teacher initially should reinforce the student for each instance of cooperation and ensure that the reinforcer is a "big deal." However, as the student begins to demonstrate an increase in cooperation, the frequency and intensity of the reinforcer can be decreased. Eventually, the teacher can implement a natural schedule of reinforcement.

In a similar fashion, if a teacher's goal is to get a group of students to use more appropriate social skills, it is advisable to provide (extra) reinforcement frequently. As the students start to improve, the artificial schedule of reinforcement can be reduced. Eventually, the teacher will want the students to be reinforced only as often as is natural. Unfortunately, some students are rarely reinforced for showing appropriate social skills, and in these cases, teachers may need to occasionally provide some additional positive feedback.

Thus, in general, when teachers begin a new program, it is advisable to provide the student with considerable reinforcement

(Skinner, 1969). As the program progresses and the student makes significant gains, the teacher can begin to slowly reduce how often the student is reinforced. Ultimately, it is desirable to fade to a naturally occurring schedule of reinforcement. As the schedule of reinforcement is faded, teachers should also reduce their reliance on artificial reinforcers and move to natural reinforcers.

8

Punishment

> *Before considering use of a punishment-based program, the educational staff should attempt to alter the behavior using a positive reinforcement approach.*

Based on research conducted over many decades, a technology of procedures that can be used to directly reduce disruptive behaviors has been established (Favell & Reid, 1988; Lovaas & Simmons, 1969). Most often, these procedures are based on the principle known as punishment. *Punishment,* typically, is the application of a punisher following the display of an inappropriate or disruptive behavior. In the last decade, the use of punishment has become the central point of many discussions between professionals who either consider the use of punishment unethical on any grounds and others who consider punishment as a viable technology that can, when properly used, help to reduce very undesirable behaviors and help students to learn (see Alberto & Troutman, 1990; Tawney & Gast, 1984).

Many professionals argue against the use of behavior management programs and, in particular, against the use of intervention programs that involve punishment. The focus of this book is not to argue whether punishment is morally right or wrong, but to present intervention principles and procedures that have been shown to be highly effective in helping students to become more cooperative and less disruptive. Any procedure, whether it is based on the principles of punishment or reinforcement, can be misused or used to exert unneeded influence over others. Being knowledgeable about these procedures is the first step each person must take before deciding whether they feel comfortable in using them while they work with students.

DEFINING A PUNISHER

A *punisher* is a consequent stimulus that decreases the future rate or probability of occurrence of the target behavior and is administered contingently on the production of the undesired or inappropriate behavior (Azrin & Holz, 1966). In other words, a punisher is an event or item that is delivered to the student contingent on the display of an inappropriate behavior and that decreases the likelihood that the student will show the disruptive behavior again. Thus, when discussing punishers, it is important to consider the function that punishers have in relation to a target behavior. That function is to decrease the undesirable, disruptive behavior.

Common Forms of Punishers

As with the use of reinforcers, punishers may vary substantially from student to student and take many forms (Bailey, 1983). It is well beyond the scope of this book to list and review all of the documented (and ethical) forms of punishers. Instead, the principles of punishment are presented in light of punishers that are often used in educational settings.

For instance, I have seen many teachers say "no" to students after they have shown a disruptive behavior. Saying no to a student may serve as a punisher, if it decreases the student's display of an inappropriate disruptive behavior. Giving a student a frown may serve as a punisher. I worked with one student who would immediately stop being disruptive if his teacher gave him a frown. For him, a frown served as a strong punisher and could be used to discourage mildly disruptive behaviors. Another teacher reported that shaking her head from side to side served as an effective punisher.

As with reinforcers, the use of punishers must be individualized for each student. What serves as a punisher for one student may not be a punisher for another. Furthermore, a "punitive" event, such as going to the principal's or counselor's office, may not serve as a punisher for a particular student, even though it is intended to serve as a strong corrective measure. In fact, one assistant school principal reported to me that more and more students were being sent to the school counselor's office. After investigating this concern, it appeared that the students were intentionally acting up to go see the counselor, because the counselor was considered a "good guy" by the students. The counselor and the assistant principal designed a program that involved allowing the students to earn "extra time" with the counselor by displaying appropriate classroom behaviors. Of course, the counselor continued to handle the emergency cases, as needed.

In a similar manner, it is possible that a "pleasant" event for one student may actually serve as a punisher for another student. For instance, although many young students like their parents to join them for lunch in the school cafeteria, other students may become embarrassed and not want their parents to come for lunch. The bottom line is that great care must be taken when implementing a punishment-based program.

GENERAL GUIDELINES

When a teacher decides to incorporate the principle of punishment in an intervention program, a few general guidelines should be followed. These guidelines are based on research reported in the literature (Alberto & Troutman, 1990). As with any procedure, it is important for professionals to keep up with the refinements developed by researchers as time goes on.

Be Consistent
   The contingency must be delivered in a consistent manner. For example, if a teacher is going to send a student to "the bench" for initiating fights with others during recess, the teacher must implement this procedure consistently. If the student is only sent to the bench every so often, it is unlikely that the student will learn not to initiate fights.

Be Direct and to the Point
   If social disapproval is part of the punisher, the adult should be direct and to the point. For example, if a

young boy is found kicking another boy while lining up to come inside the classroom, the adult should simply state: "No kicking other students," and if needed apply some other contingency, such as having the boy sit on the bench for a brief period of time.

Keep It Brief

If the student has a history of being disruptive for attention, the teacher should not provide the student with long and involved discussions or lectures as to why it is not right to kick someone else. Providing the student with long one-to-one discussions after being disruptive may serve as a reinforcer rather than a punisher, and promote such behavior. I have always suggested that if teachers want to provide "lectures" to students, they should provide them contingent on the student's display of appropriate behaviors and ensure that they are positive behaviors.

Be Firm, But Don't Get Upset

Yelling, venting frustrations, and clearly becoming upset with students is not part of punishment. If a teacher uses socially disapproving statements, such as "no," to attempt to reduce a student's disruptive behavior, the teacher must remain calm, yet firm. Teachers have reported that when they have almost lost their tempers, the student's disruptive behavior actually began to worsen, rather than improve. Being emotionally upset and showing this to your students may be counterproductive. For example, a newly credentialed teacher described a situation that occurred with one of her students. The teacher began to yell at a student for making a large mess. Although the student stopped, the teacher said that she felt out of control and guilty that she had yelled at her student. She further recognized that yelling was not the best way to have handled the situation when other students in the class began to yell at students who became disruptive. Although students may need corrective feedback, the manner in which it is delivered is also important.

Do Not Increase the Intensity of a Punisher Slowly

If a mild punisher, such as saying "no" in a whisper, does not work, the teacher should not increase the intensity of the punisher slowly. Doing so may only serve to teach the student to accept more and more intense punishers. It is vital that the teacher attempts to "match" the level of the disruptive behavior with a functional punisher of similar strength on an individualized basis for each student.

Nip the Behavior in the Bud
Waiting for a relatively long period of time after a student begins to be disruptive may make it harder for the teacher to stop the behavior. For instance, if a student begins to show some minor tantrums and disruptive behaviors, such as stomping his feet and saying phrases such as "No, I will not stop, you can't make me," waiting until it becomes worse may make it harder to stop the behavior. The only exception is that if the teacher is correctly implementing the procedure of planned ignoring, as discussed in Chapter 15.

Use the Least Aversive Stimulus That Works
Related to the last two considerations is the rule that a teacher should use the least aversive stimulus that works to reduce the undesirable disruptive behavior. Typically, a teacher has a predetermined list of possible punishers that may be implemented in her classroom, as reviewed and approved by significant other adults. As part of classroom management program, there may be set contingencies for a student's display of various disruptive behaviors. The contingencies often vary depending on the severity of the disruptive behavior and whether it is the first or repeated occurence of the behavior.

Aside from the general guidelines just presented, it is mandatory for teachers and instructional assistants to follow their system's guidelines and ensure that they have support from their supervisors and colleagues. Even though the literature supports the use of a certain punishment-based procedure, teachers must understand that they are working within a system with an established set of rules and regulations. If a teacher feels strongly about implementing a program that is counter to the established guidelines, the teacher should work with the department chair or supervisor. Having the support of a supervisor is important whenever a teacher varies from the system's traditional practices.

As previously mentioned, to use or not to use punishment is one of the most hotly debated topics among researchers, psychologists, teachers, and administrators. One side states that using punishment is unethical, demoralizing, and not needed; the other states that it is important to consider whether there is an empirical and clinical need to implement a punishment-based program. The proper question may actually be: What are the acceptable forms of punishment that can be implemented in a classroom?

PART V

METHODS OF INCREASING COOPERATIVE CLASSROOM BEHAVIORS

Teaching students to use positive and productive classroom skills is often the best way to decrease behavior problems.

A positive reinforcement approach can be used to teach academic skills, increase homework completion, improve daily living skills, and promote cooperative classroom behaviors. Central to this book is the idea that teachers and other classroom personnel should emphasize a systematic approach to increasing positive classroom behaviors and decreasing classroom behavior problems. A number of intervention and classroom management programs have been developed based on the principle of positive reinforcement. These programs are designed to promote appropriate classroom behaviors while reducing disruptive behaviors. The strength of this approach is that it can be used not only to decrease inappropriate behaviors, but also to strengthen a student's use of cooperative and productive classroom skills.

In this section, commonly used programs based on positive reinforcement are presented. The first program, which incorporates the principles of partial participation, focuses on increasing a student's cooperation and instruction following. The second approach, often referred to as a token economy program, uses the principles of generalized condition reinforcers and back-up reinforcers. The third approach, known as teacher-student contracts, is based, in part, on shared control. The fourth approach presented is relatively new and is known as self-monitoring or self-management programs. These programs teach the student to monitor the occurrence of the (positive) target behavior. The fifth strategy focuses on increasing effective communication skills in students whose disruptive behaviors result from difficulty in effectively communicating their wants, desires, and needs.

9

Maximizing Student Cooperation

Cooperation forms the basis and the starting point for effective interactions between a teacher and a student.

Having a cooperative relationship with a student forms the basis of learning and reduces the likelihood of the student being disruptive (Parrish, Cataldo, Kolko, Neef, & Egel, 1986). If a student does not cooperate, a teacher will have very little success in teaching the student. Although some teachers assume that students will be cooperative, students often exhibit varying degrees of noncompliance.

A large percentage of the cases in which I have served as a consultant have involved the issue of compliance. A student does not follow the directions or requests given by the teacher or the instructional assistant. A student has "difficulty" with the classroom rules, such as remaining quiet during daily opening activities. A student's level of cooperation varies depending on the type of request, the subject matter, the situation, and the adult involved.

Regardless of the student, there is a sequence of activities that is usually conducted to design an individualized program to increase cooperation with the student. These general activities include the following.

COLLECTION OF A-B-C DATA

Using this method of data collection, the teacher delineates the situations in which the student is noncompliant. Rather than simply reporting that "the student is noncompliant," the teacher must determine when the student is more and less likely to be cooperative. It is likely that the student is noncompliant in certain situations, and it is vital to specify those situations. The teacher must note what precedes noncompliant behavior in terms of:

- The situation and/or activity
- The request being given
- The person who gave the request

In addition to the antecedents of the behavior, the teacher must determine what events occur after the student is noncompliant. For example, the student may escape a work-related request, such as "Clean up those blocks and get ready for math," or receive much attention from the teacher or other students. For example, Johnny, a five-year-old student, was reported as being very noncompliant and disruptive. Based on the A–B–C data gathered by the teacher, it became apparent that he received much attention following each noncompliant act in the form of lectures from the teaching staff and being laughed at by the other students.

In addition to clearly defining the antecedents and consequences of the behavior, the teacher must formally define the exact form of the noncompliance. Noncompliance may occur in the form of actively doing the opposite of what was requested by a teacher. Noncompliance may also be defined as occurring in the form of a student passively not following through with a teacher's request and continuing with a previous activity. Other teachers have noncompliant students who are described as eventually following through with the request, but taking too long to initiate the response, or complying only after the teacher has repeated the request several times. Clearly defining the form of noncompliance helps the teacher plan an appropriate and effective intervention program.

From the A–B–C data, the teacher will know what situations are most likely to produce noncompliant behavior, what form of noncompliance the student typically shows, and what type of consequences may have influenced the students' display of noncompliance. These data are used to develop an individualized intervention program.

SPECIFY THE RULES

Compliance typically is defined in relation to a student not following a rule or a particular request. However, before a student can be expected to comply with a request or a rule, the teacher and other school staff must agree on what the rules are. Although hundreds of rules exist, some very formally defined by the teacher, school system, or even our society, it is usually advantageous for a teacher to have a relatively small, yet vital, number of rules. Having a small number of rules helps to emphasize their importance.

After the teacher, instructional assistant, (and administrators) have agreed on the initial list of rules, the rules must be clearly communicated to the students. For students who have "no diagnoses" and function within the "normal range," communicating the rules may simply involve presenting them along with examples.

One question teachers frequently ask is whether the rules should be stated in a positive manner or negative manner. For instance, a rule requiring students to raise their hands to answer questions may be stated: "After the question is presented, the students will raise a hand to be called on" or "After the question is presented, the students must not call out the answer." In general, stating rules in a positive manner is preferred. Positive statements allow the teacher many opportunities to reinforce students for showing positive behaviors and for following the rules. In addition, for students who benefit from modeling, positive statement and reinforcement of the rules enable them to observe their peers being reinforced for following the rules and demonstrating positive behaviors.

To remind the students of the rules, teachers often find it useful to post the rules in the classroom. Posting the rules cues the students to follow them and reminds the teacher to enforce them. If the teacher is working with a class of youngsters who have a history of noncompliant behavior, a teacher may need to review the rules with the students on a regular basis, especially if the class is doing a great job following the rules.

SPECIFY THE CONSEQUENCES

In addition to specifying the rules, it is important that the consequences are understood by all students. Again, teachers should meet with other important individuals, such as psychologists and administrators, to receive input and to agree on the type of consequences that can be used in the class and school prior to the initiation of a behavior management program. In programs based on positive reinforcement, consequences must be reinforcing for the students, and they must be developed with this in mind. If a teacher delineates a list of "positive reinforcers" without either direct or indirect input from the students, the teacher runs the risk of incorporating items or activities that will not serve as true reinforcers.

After the consequences have been delineated, the students should be made aware of them. This can be done by listing the consequences on the board (near the rules) or by reviewing the consequences with students. Most importantly, the teacher's use of the consequences will help the students learn the relationship between the rules and the consequences.

During the initial portion of the intervention program, it is especially important for adults to implement the consequences in a highly consistent manner. For example, a student named Thomas had a history of not following through with requests without dawdling for 5 to 10 minutes. Thomas was being served by three different teachers. As part of the intervention program to reduce his dawdling, all of the adults who were working with Thomas had to consistently reinforce him for responding to requests without dawdling. Because the reinforcer consisted of positive social praise, each teacher had to provide Thomas with positive social praise contingent on his relatively quick responding. Reinforcing Thomas on a fairly frequent basis during the initial portion of the program helped Thomas to learn to begin his work without dawdling.

CATCH THEM BEING COOPERATIVE

One of the most powerful, yet simplest, procedures to increase cooperation is to catch the student cooperating and encourage his or her good behavior. Teaching students how to be cooperative involves reinforcing them for being cooperative. If praise is used, teachers must remember to praise the student when the student is cooperating. All too often, teachers (and others, including myself) forget to praise students when they are cooperating and catch them only when they are being noncompliant. If a student gets extra attention only for being noncompliant, the punitive lecture that follows the noncompliance may actually serve as a reinforcer in the form of added attention for the student.

During the initial portion of an intervention program, teachers should pay a little extra attention to the students when they are following general rules such as putting up their chairs at the end of the day, as illustrated in Figure 9-1. Rather than providing a student with a one-to-one lecture following noncompliance, provide him with one-to-one praise after he shows positive behavior and cooperation. The following general guidelines are often used.

1. *Praise the student immediately* when the student is following through with a request or upholding a rule posted in the classroom such as working quietly, playing with other students cooperatively, or completing an independent assignment. Typically, when you praise the student, state exactly what the stu-

Figure 9-1. *Catching students who are following the class rules is a powerful method of promoting cooperation.*

dent is doing that is good. For example, "Marsha, you are working very quietly, that's great" or "Mark and Sally, you are doing a great job working together to complete the puzzle." If a token program is being used, don't forget to provide the students with a token for following through with the rules.

2. *Check on the student frequently* so that you have many chances to praise the student for good behavior and for following the posted rules. At first, an older student may need positive feedback quite often, such as every 10 minutes. As the student begins to show an increase in positive behaviors, slowly add two to three minutes at a time to how long you wait before you check again. Continue adding time slowly until you check the student only as often as you check other students who typically follow through with the established rules. With a younger student, the teacher needs to check the student more often, such as every five minutes. In an analogous manner, the teacher adds more time in smaller increments until the student clearly shows good gains in appropriate behavior.

Obviously, the frequency with which a teacher checks on a student depends on more than the student's age. The frequency should be based on data gathered prior to the introduction of the program. For instance, the frequency is based on how often the student typically is disruptive and fails to follow through with rules. Students who act up more often may need a greater frequency of reinforcement for following the rules when the intervention is first initiated. In addition, other variables, such as the task of the nature or the overall situation, should be taken into consideration.

There are several strategies to help a teacher to remember to check the student. Teachers can use a check sheet marked off with the number of times the student should be reinforced during the day or session or a list of activities or specific requests to be given to the student with space to record the student's compliance and the teacher's delivery of reinforcement. Teachers should have some method of ensuring that the student is being reinforced for following the rules.

3. *If all is going well, don't feel that you should let the student be* by ignoring calm, cooperative behaviors. Teachers often suggest that reinforcing a student interrupts the student's concentration. Although this may sometimes be true, typically, a quick pleasing smile or a whispered "you're doing very good" will serve as a reinforcer without producing a major disruption. Again, if the student gets extra attention only when misbehaving, the teacher runs the risk that the student will learn to misbehave to get extra attention.

4. *Keep your praise relatively brief* when you catch the student being cooperative. At first, students, especially younger ones, may stop their appropriate behavior and try to talk with you when you give them attention for being cooperative and appropriate. They need to be reminded that they are being praised for showing the appropriate behavior, such as playing with other students, and not for talking with you. After a brief period of time, your added attention will be less disruptive.

TRY TO GUARANTEE SUCCESS

When faced with a seemingly overwhelming problem, try to initiate an intervention plan for cooperation that virtually guarantees success for both the student and yourself. I frequently am asked to consult with a teacher who has just received a student who has a history of failing to comply with most requests. Aside from ensuring that the student follows general rules, such as those that pertain to the student's safety and well being, teachers find it difficult to know where to begin a program with such students.

With many students, it is easier to start work on cooperation when the task is not new, difficult, or a task that the student avoids like the plague. For many students, especially those with severe handicapping conditions, it is advisable to work on compliance with tasks that are either preferred by the student or well within the student's repetoire. This strategy helps to facilitate compliance and provides opportunities for the teacher to reinforce the student for compliance. As the student shows greater compliance with these tasks, the teacher can begin to incorporate less preferred tasks or tasks that are more difficult. Ensuring success from the start of an intervention program facilitates more success as the program continues.

AFTER INCREASING COOPERATION, FADE THE PROGRAM

When teachers clearly see a change in a student's level of cooperation, they often immediately stop the program. However, to the dismay of the teacher, the student's noncompliance and related disruptive behaviors frequently arise again in a relatively short period of time. To avoid this, the teacher must fade the program over time rather than stop the program all at once. Fading the program entails slowly moving from using extra attention as an reinforcer to giving the student the same amount of attention typically provided to the other students in the class.

For example, a teacher implemented a reinforcement program that involved providing a student named Trisha with extra attention during class to increase on-task performance and the completion of assignments prior to recess. As Trisha began to show a definite increase in task completion, the teacher began to fade the extra attention and, ultimately, provided Trisha with attention only when she turned in assignments and while playing with the other students during recess.

Fading to natural contingencies is also important. For example, if a teacher begins a reinforcment program for compliance with the use of edibles because no other reinforcers could be identified, the teacher eventually will need to fade the edibles rather than just stopping their use. Given the difficulty professionals have had in fading from edibles to other reinforcers, it is advisable not to overuse edibles.

SPECIAL CONSIDERATIONS

Given the wide variety of students who show problems in cooperation, individualized procedures must be defined to fit the particular students' needs and the situation. The procedures just noted help teachers to increase students' cooperation while concurrently reducing displays of many disruptive behaviors. These procedures must be implemented by those professionals who are properly trained and who can correctly monitor the implementation of their programs.

10

Token Economy Programs

A token economy program allows students to learn that good behaviors lead to reinforcement and disruptive behaviors lead to being fined.

One of the most commonly used behavior management systems is the Token Economy Program (Kazdin, 1977). In general, a token economy system is a program that is based on economics. As part of a token economy program, a student earns tokens (rather than money, in most cases) for displaying a wide variety of appropriate classroom behaviors including task completion, responding to instructions, and playing appropriately with others. The tokens are acquired contingently and immediately after students display such behaviors. The tokens can be used at a later time to purchase preferred items in a reinforcement store, to obtain more time playing a favorite computer game, or to participate in an extracurricular activity such as an outing. In addition, in many token programs, a student can lose tokens for displaying disruptive behaviors or for not cooperating with the teacher.

The implementation of a token program is analogous to the use of money in the "real world." Money can be earned and spent to participate in preferred activities or to obtain highly desired objects. In addition, just like in the real world, if a student breaks a rule, the student can be fined and lose some number of tokens. A token system can be used with individual students or a group of students. Because each student can earn, spend, and lose tokens in an individualized manner, a token program enables a teacher to implement a single program that can have a dramatic effect on an entire class of students. Another advantage of a token program is that it can be implemented with only certain behaviors or used to simultaneously target a relatively large number of cooperative and disruptive behaviors.

MAJOR COMPONENTS OF A TOKEN PROGRAM

The Token Reinforcers

Obviously, to have a token program, a teacher must have some relatively small tokens or other objects that can be exchanged with the students. Typically, teachers use chips (also known as poker chips), buttons, washers, and marbles. In choosing a token, it is important to choose something that is not easily accessible to the student outside of the classroom (just in case the student gets the idea of making counterfeit tokens). In addition, tokens should be durable.

Students also need a place to save the tokens. Teachers often use small cloth bags or plastic jars if the tokens are chips, marbles, or similar objects. Teachers who implement pegs use a pegboard. Teachers who use play money use envelopes or some type of "homemade" wallets. If stars are being given, a simple sheet of paper is sufficient. In a similar manner, the classroom blackboard can be used for hand-drawn checks or stars.

One last consideration is ensuring that the tokens pose no harm to a student. Although this is usually not a problem, students have been known to ingest such items. Other students have thrown their tokens during a tantrum. Teachers should avoid the use of hard tokens, such as marbles, if this is a possibility with their students.

Listing Positive Behaviors

Tokens should be provided to the students contingent on their display of appropriate and cooperative behavior. They should be told what behaviors will be reinforced. In fact, some teachers ask students to participate in forming (or at least adding to) the list of positive behaviors. In general, when selecting behaviors to be targeted, the following should be considered:

- Start with a small number of target behaviors that students can accomplish with relatively little effort.
- Have a set criteria for each behavior to ensure objectivity in reinforcing the student and to facilitate the student's understanding of what behaviors will be reinforced.
- Include only behaviors that can clearly be observed and measured.

In addition to determining what behaviors will be reinforced, the teacher also needs to decide on the "payoff" for each occurrence of the positive behaviors. In a sense, the state of the economy must be set. To accomplish this task, the teacher should prioritize the target behaviors and take into consideration the frequency with which the students will have opportunities to receive a token. If the economy is set too high, providing a large payoff for most behaviors, the students may become satiated with the tokens. If the economy is set too low, and the back-up reinforcers are very costly, students may lose motivation to work over an extended period of time to obtain enough tokens. In addition, if too many tokens are circulating, additional problems, such as students losing them, may be created. It is very important to set the value of the payoff in relation to the cost of the back-up reinforcers. After deciding the value of the payoff, it should be posted along with the positive behavior.

Back-up Reinforcers

In a token reinforcement program, tokens are valued by a student, in part, because the student can exchange them for a desired item or for the opportunity to participate in a desired activity. Items may include comics, small games, grab bag items, or other preferred objects that can be incorporated into the program. Activities may include receiving extra time on a computer, going to a fast food restaurant, attending a special event, or having more time to listen to music.

Because students will earn tokens at varying rates, a fairly wide range of back-up reinforcers should be available. The important aspect of these items is that they are preferred by the students. If the teacher arbitrarily chooses items and events, he or she runs the risk that the students may not want to work to obtain them. On the other hand, items and events that will not break the teacher's or the classroom's bank should be chosen.

During the initial implementation of a token system, less costly items or activities should be available to allow students to experience the excitement of turning their tokens in for a back-up reinforcer. Less costly items can include little trinkets, secondhand toys, or a few extra minutes to use the computer. Posting a list of the back-up reinforcers along with their costs will also increase students' interest in participating in the program.

A Plan to Exchange Tokens

Opportunities for the students to exchange their tokens for back-up reinforcers should be regularly scheduled. Teachers who have a group of students with a history of exhibiting relatively high levels of disruptive behaviors should schedule fairly frequent opportunities for the students to exchange their tokens. For instance, with a class of behaviorally disordered students, Mr. Goldstein initially gave the students an opportunity to exchange their tokens for a back-up reinforcer at the end of each half day. During this initial phase, the back-up reinforcers were relatively small in comparison to those that the students were earning after a week of receiving a considerable number of tokens.

Removing Tokens for Disruptive Behavior

As part of many token programs, teachers have a fine for a student's display of disruptive and noncompliant behavior (Kazdin & Bootzin, 1972). If a student exhibits a particular disruptive behavior, it costs the student a certain number of tokens. As with the positive behaviors, the disruptive behaviors should be very well defined, observable, and measurable. The ratio of relative loss of tokens must be established in conjunction with the reward system and the cost of the back-up reinforcers.

A student must have tokens in order to lose tokens when the student is disruptive. If a teacher does not catch the student following the positive rules and does not provide him with tokens during the day, the teacher will not be able to fine the student. This is a serious problem. If a student has no tokens, then the student may feel there is nothing to lose if he acts up in the future. A teacher should avoid this situation by ensuring that students initially are provided with tokens, even though the relative importance of their positive behaviors is not great. For instance, reinforcing a student for being on task for very small periods of time rather than waiting to reinforce the student after a complete session is over may be warranted in the beginning of a program.

FADING THE PROGRAM

Prior to initiating the program, the need to eventually fade the program must be considered. The overall goal of a token program is to alter students' behaviors and to promote a more positive learning environment. However, as with any intervention program, the program must be faded in a systematic manner to eventually employ only naturally occuring contingencies.

A teacher must have a formal plan to fade students' involvement in the token reinforcement system (LaNunziata, Hunt, & Cooper, 1984). This is often accomplished by fading the number of opportunities for students to exchange their tokens. Other teachers fade their programs by switching from small items to larger items that take a relatively long time to earn. As the program evolves, the teacher must continue to rely on the use of other more naturally occurring reinforcers such as incorporating preferred tasks and topics into lesson plans. In addition, teachers must not forget to provide students with positive social approval for a job well done or for following through with classroom rules.

The following guidelines should be considered when forming a plan to fade a token economy program.

- Tokens should be delivered with social praise, and the presence of the tokens should be faded slowly.
- The criteria for earning tokens should be gradually increased.
- The number of opportunities for students to exchange their tokens for back-up reinforcers should be systematically reduced.
- The relative value and cost of the back-up reinforcers should be gradually increased.

- The back-up reinforcers eventually should include items or events are found in other settings that the students are involved in or will be involved in such as "next year's classroom."

In summary, a token economy system is a valuable method for promoting positive classroom skills and decreasing disruptive and noncompliant behaviors. This strategy can be used with an individual student or a group of students. However, considerable planning is necessary to ensure that such a program is effectively initiated, maintained, and eventually faded. Given the importance of implementing the program correctly, the following points should be reviewed.

GUIDELINES FOR IMPLEMENTING A TOKEN ECONOMY PROGRAM

1. The program should emphasize behaviors that are considered positive (e.g., task completion with neatness, appropriate social interactions, and remaining in seat).
2. Initially, students should be rewarded for the positive behaviors throughout the day.
3. The amount of the reinforcement should be in direct proportion to the amount of good behavior shown during the time period (e.g., day, week), and in relation to the back-up reinforcers that are being used (e.g., extra time to play a game on the computer).
4. Students must be taught that tokens are valued. This can be done by allowing students frequent opportunities to exchange them during the initial phase.
5. Students must be taught to save tokens and to wait for increasingly longer periods of time to exchange them for a back-up reinforcer.
6. A token economy program may need to be individualized for students with special needs.
7. If a response-cost component is added, the teacher should implement it for well-defined behaviors and ensure that the students have many opportunities to earn tokens.
8. The teacher should have a plan to fade the program.

11

Teacher-Student Contracts

A contract system involves forming a commitment between the student and the teacher.

Teacher-student contracts, also known as contingency or behavioral contracts, are viable options for helping students to exhibit more appropriate behaviors and reduce levels of disruptive behaviors (Homme, Csanyi, Gonzales, & Rechs, 1970). In this approach the student must contribute to the formation and implementation of the program and as such can help teach students to follow through with commitments. A behavioral contract typically is used on an individual basis and in reference to a particular behavior. With any contract, the two parties sit down and agree that if the student performs a certain behavior, the student will receive a specific item or opportunity to participate in an activity which serves as the reinforcer and therefore will help to motivate the student.

A behavioral contract can be made in an informal manner as in the form of a verbal agreement between a teacher and a student. For instance, Mrs. Jones, a teacher of a group of fifth graders once told me that she initiated a verbal behavioral contract between herself and a student named Bruce who had been having difficulty completing his work sheets. In particular, she said to Bruce,"After you complete your next two work sheets in a neat manner, I will give you the opportunity to choose an activity during free time." Typically, instead of being able to pick an activity during free time, Bruce had to use that time to complete his assignments. Being able to choose an activity during free time was highly valued by Bruce. After hearing the proposal, Bruce agreed and proceeded to work on his work sheets until he successfully completed them. As per the contract, Bruce was then allowed to choose an activity during free time.

In many instances, a behavioral contract is more formal and is written on paper. Having a written contract allows the student to remind him- or herself of the arrangement, rather than having to be reminded by the teacher. A written contract can require the student to behave in a prescribed manner for a period of time such as a day, week, or even a month. However, a month (or even a week) is often too long for a student to wait. It is advisable to begin with a relatively short period of time, depending on the target behavior and the value of the reinforcer.

A written contract can also require the completion of certain tasks or activities such as bringing in completed homework. Again, rather than waiting for a large amount of work to be completed before reinforcing the student, the teacher initially should target a smaller amount of work. This increases the likelihood that the student will agree to participate in the program, as well as promotes success for the student.

FORMING A WRITTEN BEHAVIORAL CONTRACT

Although the specifics of a written behavioral contract may vary, yet be successful, some general guidelines in forming contracts include:

- The contract should specify who will do the target behavior.
- The contract should specify the behavior or task to be done in an objective and measurable manner with an inclusion of quality.
- The contract should state the frequency with which the behavior will be done by the student.
- The contract should state who will provide the reinforcer.
- The contract should state very clearly what the reinforcer will entail.
- The contract should state when the student will receive the reinforcer.

Typically, both parties (the student and teacher) sign the contract. In addition to the components just listed, some type of data collection should be included on the contract form. For example, the contract could have a square for each occurrence of the target behavior for the parties to check off together. This will further help the student to perform the desired behavior and assist the teacher in accurately assessing the student's progress.

IMPLEMENTING A WRITTEN BEHAVIORAL CONTRACT

Implementing a formal behavior contract should be done in a systematic manner. After the contract has been formed and signed, there should be ongoing monitoring of the student's progress. This can be conducted jointly by the student and the teacher. If the target behavior has been well defined and previously agreed on, there should be little, if any, dispute between the teacher and the student about whether the student has performed the target behavior.

In addition, as described in the literature, other basic intervention principles should be followed while implementing a contract system.

1. *Immediacy of Reinforcement*
   As in any reinforcement program, the student should receive the reinforcer following the completion of his part of the contract. If too much time elapses, the student may not feel that the teacher is "playing fair." In addition, if the student successfully completes his part of the contract, but becomes disruptive or does something the opposite of what the contract states prior to receiving the reinforcer, the teacher will be in a bind. By providing the student with the reinforcer immediately, the teacher can avoid this type of problem.
2. *Partial Participation*
   Beginning with an easier target behavior increases student participation in the intervention program by increasing the likelihood that the student will meet success and be reinforced. Sometimes, a teacher initially must help the student perform the target behavior, but over time, the student will be able to do more and work

more independently. With other students, a teacher may contract for the student to perform only a small amount of work to facilitate some initial success. For example, a teacher reported that he had a 10-year-old student, named Dustin, who had a long history of difficulty with penmanship. Although much of his homework was virtually illegible, some of his writing was actually quite good, if Dustin took his time and concentrated. To facilitate success for Dustin, the teacher decided to have Dustin initially do less homework, but require him to complete it neatly. If Dustin accomplished this each day, he was allowed more access to the computer in the class to play math games during free time. This was agreeable to Dustin, and it was written as a behavioral contract between the teacher and the student. (His parents also participated in this decision process.) After Dustin met success for five days, the teacher began to increase the amount of homework he had to complete neatly, and he received an increased amount of time on the computer. Ultimately, Dustin completed most of his work neatly.

3. *Clear and Concise*

    Behavioral contracts should be written clearly and concisely. No fancy jargon or legalese. Both the teacher and the student should be able to fully understand the contract. To ensure that the contract is clear to both parties, it is useful to allow the student to help write the contract. Involving students is one of the best ways to ensure that they become "committed" to following through. Students can help define the target behaviors and provide the teacher with a variety of possible reinforcers that may be incorporated into the contract. Students also can be involved in the monitoring of the obtainment of the goal stated in the contract. Forming a straightforward, well-written contract increases the likelihood of success for both the student and teacher.

4. *Emphasize the Positive Behavior*

    Contingency contracts are based on the use of positive reinforcement. The contract should emphasize the positive classroom behavior the teacher wants the student to demonstrate. For example, a contract regarding a student remaining in his seat could be written as "Joey will remain in his seat throughout the math session and then be allowed to have five minutes free time on the computer." In contrast, a poorly written contract might say, "If Joey gets out of his seat during math, he will not have five minutes free time on the computer."

In summary, behavioral contracts can be used to effectively promote positive classroom behaviors with a wide variety of students. Even with students who have problems reading and writing, teachers can use contracts by incorporating pictures and symbols. Teachers are encouraged to use the simplest contract possible. In addition to facilitating gains in the targeted behavior or skill, behavioral contracts can build strong working relationships between teachers and students, and teach students to accept more responsibility for their actions.

12

Self-Monitoring Programs

Self-monitoring programs can help improve a student's behavior as well as teach the student to become more responsible and to work more independently.

Self-monitoring, sometimes referred to as self-management, is a strategy that involves teaching the student to help the teacher implement and monitor an intervention program (Anderson-Inman, Paine, & Deutchmena, 1984; Kazdin, 1975). This rather broad strategy refers to a variety of procedures that have a common theme of involving the student in a proactive manner to help change a target behavior. The use of this strategy allows students to help the teacher to modify their behavior and to keep track of how well they are doing. Thus, this strategy helps teachers help students to help themselves. From a teacher's perspective, this approach shifts some responsibility and work from the teacher to the student. As shown in Figure 12–1, a student can work independently and monitor his task completion without much assistance from a teacher.

During the past five years, more and more teachers have incorporated self-monitoring strategies in their efforts to facilitate increases in positive behaviors while decreasing undesirable disruptive behaviors. Professionals have used this strategy to promote improved communication and social skills with children and youth.

107

Figure 12-1. *Having a student monitor his task completion can help him to remain on task and meet success.*

Teachers have applied this strategy to teach students in regular and special education classrooms to remain seated and on-task. In a similar manner, this approach has been used to increase independent completion of assignments

Further examples will be discussed, as the major components of these programs are reviewed. This chapter also discusses how a self-monitoring program is developed, implemented, and eventually faded as a student learns more appropriate classroom behaviors and study skills.

MAJOR COMPONENTS OF A SELF-MONITORING PROGRAM

Defining the Behavior

As in any intervention program, the first step in using a self-monitoring program is to clearly define the behavior or behaviors to be targeted and monitored. With this approach, the behavioral definition must be especially clear and concise to reduce problems the student might have in accurately monitoring the occurrences of the behaviors.

Initial Instruction

Some work in the area of self-monitoring suggests that this strategy is useful in facilitating initial change in behavior. However, other professionals recommend that a behavior first be directly targeted by a teacher (or other adult). After some initial change has occurred, the teacher implements the self-monitoring program to ensure that the changes maintain over time and are seen across different settings. Because the teacher is interested in increasing a positive behavior or skill, it behooves the teacher to provide some initial direct programming to ensure that the student can exhibit the behavior with relative ease. Subsequently, the teacher can implement a self-monitoring strategy to help strengthen the behavior in the student's repertoire.

For example, Mrs. Maxwell used this approach to help teach Roxane to complete her independent math assignments. The student had a history of not remaining on-task and completing the math assignments independently. Even though she typically could "do the work," Roxane would get off-task and draw little characters on pieces of scrap paper rather than remaining on-task. Thus, the target goal was defined as teaching Roxane to complete tasks independently. Initially, the teacher worked with Roxane to make sure that she could complete the math problems and was able to place an "X" in a box on a small 3 x 5-inch card to indicate that she had completed a group of five problems. After seeing that she could do the work and accurately monitor her work, Mrs. Maxwell left Roxane to complete three additional rows of problems and to self-record. She was instructed to bring the self-monitoring card and math sheet to the teacher's desk after she completed the work. If Roxane successfully completed her work and monitored it accurately, she was allowed to enjoy a favorite activity for a small period of time. The activity was drawing little characters.

Other teachers have found it useful to role play with students to help ensure that the student can perform the behavior. For instance, a teacher of a 19-year-old youth with autism was interested in teaching the student to use complete sentences while talking with other individuals. The teacher first role played with the student to ensure that he could use complete sentences during social interactions. Following the role playing, the teacher taught the student to use a "golf counter" to keep track of the number of appropriate long sentences he used while talking with other students outside of the classroom. If he exhibited a preset number of appropriate sentences during the day, he was allowed to have more time listening to his favorite music. This approach worked, although the teacher had to conduct spot checks to ensure that the student was accurately monitoring occurrences of the target behavior.

Teaching the Student to Self-Monitor

At the heart of this strategy is the need for the student to learn to monitor the behavior in a relatively independent manner. To successfully teach a student to self-monitor, several factors must be considered. There are student factors such as age, level of functioning, and prior history of being able to monitor behavior successfully. There are factors related to the target behavior such as whether the behavior is complex, or can be readily discriminated from other behaviors (especially appropriate versus inappropriate). Last, there are environmental factors, which include the degree that people in other settings support the implementation of the program and provide natural contingencies.

With a student who has little experience in self-monitoring, it is advisable to begin with the teacher overseeing the actual recording being done by the student, as shown in Figure 12–2. In addition, teachers often find it valuable to begin by having the student monitor the behavior for a relatively short period of time or for a relatively few occurrences of the behavior. This allows the teacher to ensure accuracy and the student to meet success in using this strategy.

Having the Student "Practice"

After the teacher has seen that the student can monitor the behavior accurately, the student can begin to use the self-recording system more independently (see Fig. 12–3). If the target behavior and self-monitoring is to occur in other settings, the teacher needs to validate that the student has indeed performed the target behavior and correctly used the self-monitoring program. Validation can be accomplished by asking adults who are involved with the student in other settings such as teachers, cafeteria monitors, and parents. If the student has difficulty generalizing the use of

Figure 12-2. *Initially, it is advantageous for the teacher to oversee the student's efforts to self-monitor.*

the system, the teacher can continue with the training and possibly provide "booster" sessions in some of the additional settings.

Delineating and Using a Back-up Reinforcer

Self-monitoring programs are effective for a number of reasons. Although self-monitoring alone may influence the student's display of a behavior, the addition of a positive reinforcement component substantially facilitates a positive outcome. After correctly implementing the self-monitoring strategy for a set period of time or after a set number of responses, the student should be rewarded. The reinforcement component could be in the form of receiving a point for each occurrence and using the points to purchase a back-up reinforcer, similar to a token system of reinforcement.

The reinforcement component also could be determined by having the teacher and the student decide what special activity or item the student will receive as a reinforcer after the student achieves a set goal. If, after the student achieves the goal, and he or she prefers another reinforcer of comparable value, the teacher would be wise to consider providing the student with the alternative reinforcer, if it is available. This potential problem can be avoided by offering the student a range of reinforcers, rather than deciding on a specific reinforcer prior to implementation of the program.

Fading the Program

During the last phase of a self-monitoring program, the teacher must systematically remove the program. It is vital to maintain the improvements obtained in the student's behavior while fading the program. The following are some general guidelines for successfully fading a self-monitoring program.

1. Slowly increase the length of time before the student exchanges the points for a backup program.
2. Increase the amount of work in the task until the student completes an entire assignment prior to receiving a reward.

Figure 12–3. *As the student masters the use of the self-monitoring procedure, the student should be allowed to practice independently.*

3. Shift the reinforcer to more naturally occurring reinforcers such as positive social praise and recognition.

METHODS OF SELF-MONITORING

Methods of self-monitoring are as numerous as the behaviors that can be targeted using this strategy. In general, however, the following methods are typically used by teachers.

Tally Method

One of the easiest self-monitoring methods is to have a student tally the occurrences of a particular behavior during a period of time. The student tallies each occurrence of the behavior on a separate sheet or small card. The student can carry the card, which permits the student to work on the target behavior across settings.

Marking Task Completion on a Worksheet

Some teachers prefer to have the student mark task completion on the sheet of paper that is part of the task. Instead of using a small card to record the completion of math problems, the teacher could have a small box at the end of each row of problems. After the student completes the row, the student would place an "X" in the box. This method is very easy to use and can readily be faded. As the student improves, the number of problems before the student is to record an "X" can be increased.

Wrist Counters

A popular method used to self-monitor a single behavior is the use of a wrist counter. A wrist counter allows a student to self-monitor discretely. The counter resembles a watch and has a small "stem" or button that the student pushes to record the occurrences of the target behavior. The display on the face of the counter is the total number of occurrences.

A Penny for Each Occurrence

A method that is sometimes used with students who want to be relatively covert in monitoring a behavior involves having the student take a small object, such as a penny, out of one pocket and place it in another pocket. For example, each time a student initiated an appropriate social behavior, he transferred a penny from his left coat pocket to his left pants pocket. Following a set time period, he counted the number of pennies and recorded the number of appropriate social behaviors. If the number of occurrences is very high, the teacher may want to use another method.

13

Teaching Communication Skills

Students who have difficulty communicating with others may display disruptive behaviors in an effort to communicate.

As previously mentioned, some students' disruptive behaviors serve a communicative function (Carr, 1988; Carr & Durand, 1985). Rather than implementing a punishment-based program to reduce these behaviors, and the student's effort to communicate, it is preferable to implement a positive reinforcement program with a focus on teaching these students alternative and more appropriate methods of communication. Teaching a student to communicate effectively has been shown to be a successful method to reduce disruptive behaviors that serve a communicative function. This strategy is particularly useful for children with severe or profound developmental disabilities and small repertoires of appropriate communicative behaviors. If an individual has few appropriate communicative behaviors, it increases the likelihood that he or she will resort to other, less appropriate behaviors to use in his or her attempts to communicate.

Rather than targeting speech, the production of communicative utterances, or language, such as the child's vocabulary, many professionals suggest that teachers target communicative behavior. The term communicative behavior encompasses as many forms of communication — speech, sign language, gestures, picture cards, or written words. The actual form of the communicative behavior is secondary to the idea that the teacher needs to increase an appropriate form of communication that the student can use in place of an appropriate behavior. As is further described below, the form of communication must be individualized for each student.

COMPONENTS OF AN EFFECTIVE COMMUNICATION PROGRAM

Although there are a wide variety of intervention programs for students who have severe difficulties communicating with others, there is a general strategy that many teachers have found effective and easy to implement. This strategy is based on the "Natural Language Teaching Paradigm" (Koegel, O'Dell, & Koegel, 1987) and incorporates many of the basic intervention principles already discussed such as shared control, task variation, and direct/natural reinforcement.

This approach can be used to teach a wide variety of children different methods of communication, whether the form of communication is speech, sign language, gestures, or pictures. Each of the major components of this approach is presented in this chapter along with several examples of the application of each component with students.

Multiple Exemplars

As part of this approach, a teacher uses multiple exemplars to facilitate the student's acquisition of a new concept. The exemplars may be objects, tasks, activities, or use of materials, depending on the concept being taught to the student. In general, exemplars should be chosen based on their occurrence in the student's natural settings.

For example, Mr. Mann used this approach in working with a 10-year-old boy with mental retardation and severe behavior disorders. The student typically threw tantrums to obtain items or to gain access to preferred events. Because this student had considerable difficulty in communicating his needs in an appropriate manner, Mr. Mann (and the other team members) decided that it would be advantageous to teach him an efficient method of making requests. Using a total communication approach (sign and verbal components), the teacher taught the student to sign "more" while incorporating a wide variety of (preferred) objects and activities. Incorporating many exemplars helped this student to learn that the general concept of "more" could be communicated by exhibiting a sign.

Task Variation

Task variation is the process of incorporating both mastered tasks and new tasks intermittently during a teaching session (Dunlap, 1984). Mastered tasks are tasks the student has already acquired. For many students, the variation occurs on a very frequent basis, with the teacher incorporating several different tasks during the same session. This process is beneficial because it allows a student to meet considerable success while learning new tasks. Based on systematic research, the following are some steps that, when followed, will help a teacher implement this procedure.

1. The teacher selects the new task(s) to be taught. The task should be chosen based on the curriculum being used with the student.
2. The teacher selects several tasks the student has already learned that can logically be interspersed while teaching the new tasks.
3. The teacher begins to teach the new tasks, while liberally interspersing the previously acquired tasks.
4. The teacher provides the student with reinforcement contingent on responding to both the previously acquired tasks and the new tasks.

Mrs. Slate, a speech-language therapist, incorporated this strategy while teaching a student new vocabulary items. Specifically, after the student acquired a new set of vocabulary items, she retained some to be interspersed with each future set of words. This allowed the student to meet greater success and to review the previously acquired words in subsequent sessions.

Mr. Hopkins also used this strategy while teaching a group of students who had for two years failed to learn to read using standard teaching strategies. As a result of their previous failures, the group of students had a history of being disruptive during reading to avoid the task. Mr. Hopkins used a desktop publishing computer system to write some (very) short stories that incorporated the words the students had previously mastered. The blank pages in the book were then filled in by the students. Because the students knew most of the words, they experienced success. After finally meeting success in reading a "whole book," the students' motivation was increased and they began to attempt to learn to read additional words. (Incorporating their drawings also added to their motivation and commitment for reading "their book.") Using the principle of task variation while teaching communication (and other) skills increases the rate of acquisition as well as promotes greater motivation for the student to remain on-task.

Reinforcing Attempts

As normally developing children acquire communication skills, they often are provided with (natural) reinforcement for their efforts even when their productions are not entirely correct. The concept of reinforcing a student who is truly attemting to communicate is not new; however, it is often underused. Reinforcing a student for attempting to communicate increases the probability that the student will attempt to communicate (appropriately) more often. If the student attempts to communicate appropriately more often, it increases the likelihood that student will meet greater success and will not need to use disruptive behaviors to communicate with others.

Promotion of Shared Control

Research has shown that if a teacher allows the student to have some choice in what to work on, the student will show relatively more rapid improvements in communication. For children with severe or profound retardation, the task materials can include favorite objects such as special toys, games, and food snacks. With children whose problems are less severe, teachers initially can use preferred objects but eventually incorporate less concrete concepts or topics. For children who only have some difficulties communicating, teachers can attempt to increase appropriate communication skills by incorporating preferred topics of discussion. Focusing discussion on a preferred topic helps to ensure that the student remains on task with fewer direct prompts from the teacher.

The central idea of shared control is that motivation is an important variable and that allowing the student to choose the material or topic helps to facilitate positive changes by motivating the student. Often, the principle of shared control is incorporated by offering the student a box of tasks or a list of possible assignments. Having a varied, yet limited, number of possible choices involves the student and promotes greater display of positive behaviors.

Direct Reinforcement

As previously defined, direct reinforcement involves incorporating reinforcers that are directly related to the task. In teaching communication skills, a direct reinforcer is usually the referent of the vocabulary item that is being taught. For instance, if a teacher is attempting to teach a student an appropriate method to request objects, the teacher would incorporate items or activities that are preferred and provide them to the student after the student appropriately requests them.

PROGRAM IMPLEMENTATION

Implementing a program to produce an increase in effective communication skills traditionally has involved working with the student in a one-to-one manner in a relatively small treatment room. Although this approach has resulted in improving the communication skills of many students with mild to severe needs, teachers have often reported that the treatment changes do not transfer to other settings. In recent years, professionals have begun to implement an integrated model of communication programming.

In accordance with this strategy, teachers promote the student's acquisition and generalization of communication skills. Typically their efforts are coordinated by a trained speech-language therapist, as needed, and are supplemented with one-to-one intervention provided by the therapist. Teachers and other professionals ultimately must ask whether the approach they use for a student addresses the individual needs of the student.

PART VI

Methods of Decreasing Disruptive Classroom Behaviors

> *Although there are many techniques designed to decrease disruptive behaviors, some are more preferred and accepted by teachers, parents, and administrators.*

In addition to the techniques discussed in the last section, there is another group of procedures that can be used to effectively and directly reduce a student's display of classroom behavior problems. This section describes methods that can be easily implemented in an educational setting by teachers and other trained professionals. Although there are other techniques that are as effective, if not more effective, in decreasing unwanted behaviors, the incorporation of the procedures described in this section is, in part, based on preferences expressed by teachers, parents, and administrators.

Incorporation of the following procedures in a student's educational program must be done by individuals who have been trained to a criterion level in correctly using them. Aside from the first technique, which involves teaching the student an alternative behavior that serves the same function as the disruptive behavior, the other procedures involve contingencies that are often viewed as unpleasant. These techniques include: planned ignoring, time-out, response cost, and fixing the environment. Prior to using these techniques, teachers are strongly encouraged to implement a program based on positive reinforcement. However, if a program based solely on positive reinforcement does not work, these techniques may be incorporated into the program to promote reductions in disruptive behaviors. As previously indicated, teachers need to collect data on the implementation of treatment programs and to objectively assess the need to introduce the following procedures. In addition, implementation of these procedures must be done in accordance with the policies of the school system.

14

Increasing Other Behaviors That Serve the Same Function

> *Rather than punishing a disruptive behavior, teachers can increase another behavior that serves the same function, thereby reducing the likelihood that the student will continue to be disruptive.*

DETERMINING THE FUNCTION OF A BEHAVIOR

Based on A–B–C data, a teacher can determine what function the disruptive behavior serves for the student. After determining the function the behavior serves, the teacher can form an intervention program that emphasizes teaching the student an alternative behavior that will serve the same function (Carr, 1988). For example, if a student typically yells to get the teacher's attention, the teacher can provide attention to the student contingent on the student raising his hand. Great care must therefore be taken to accurately delineate the function of the disruptive behavior.

For example, Mr. Brown reported a case involving a 9-year-old student in a class for behaviorally disordered children. Mr. Brown had become very concerned with the student's increasing display of minor verbal aggressive episodes. Mr. Brown and his teaching assistant first collected A–B–C data and determined that

123

124 ≡ METHODS OF DECREASING DISRUPTIVE BEHAVIORS

the student was exhibiting verbal outbursts towards other students to initiate social interactions. Through further observations, the teacher discovered that this student rarely initiated interactions with others, as other students typically do, as illustrated in Figure 14–1. Rather than punishing the student for his display of the relatively mild outbursts, the staff decided that it would be advantageous to teach the student appropriate social skills. Based on observations of other students of the same age, the teacher formed a list of specific phrases they commonly used to initiate interactions. The teacher and assistant then proceeded to closely observe the student and to reinforce him for any attempt to initiate appropriate social interactions. In addition, they often modeled the appropriate methods of initiating social interactions. They also provided the student with gentle encouragement to try some of these appropriate skills. As the student began to use these new social skills, the student's reliance on using the disruptive behaviors subsided. Mr. Brown further noted that the student be-

Figure 14–1. *Reinforcing appropriate social skills can help to eliminate disruptive behaviors.*

came more popular with other classmates and his parents even noticed a change in the way he interacted with his siblings.

The effects of this strategy can be quite powerful. It is based on a long line of research conducted by numerous professionals who have sought to refine positive strategies to decrease disruptive behaviors. It is similar to "Catch Them Being Cooperative or Good," but also incorporates information from the A–B–C assessment to delineate the function of the behavior. This approach is particularly useful when working with a student who exhibits relatively minor disruptive behavior.

GENERAL CONSIDERATIONS

Several issues need to be considered before using this approach with a student.

How long has the student shown the disruptive behavior? Although this approach is applicable for both young and older students, it is especially effective for students who do not have a long history of exhibiting disruptive behaviors. If the disruptive behavior has been serving a function for the student for a relatively long time, it may be more difficult to teach the student an alternate behavior.

Can the disruptive behavior be tolerated? If a student shows disruptive behaviors that place (or potentially place) the student or others at risk of being hurt, this approach may not be appropriate. Because reduction of the disruptive behavior is based on the teacher teaching the student an alternative behavior, this approach may take some time. In this situation, the teacher should use another strategy or combine this procedure with others to form a more comprehensive and efficient intervention.

Does the student continue to use the disruptive behavior? This concern pertains to whether the student attempts to continue to use the disruptive behavior in the same manner while he learns to use the positive behavior. Even though a student is learning a positive skill such as appropriate initiations, this does not always guarantee that the disruptive behavior will be reduced. Some students alternate between the two behaviors or display both concurrently. To facilitate reduction in the inappropriate behavior, it is advisable not to allow that behavior to be functional for the student. For example, if a student has a history of getting extra attention for whining, the teacher should not provide the student with attention while he is whining, but only when the student shows a positive attention-getting behavior. Again, the teacher must decide ahead of time whether it is possible to make the disruptive behavior "nonfunctional."

As in any intervention program, being consistent is crucial. Once a teacher decides to provide reinforcement for a positive behavior and not for another behavior, the teacher must be as consistent as possible in implementing the program. With a high level of consistency, teaching a student an alternative behavior that serves the same function has a greater probability of being an effective approach.

15

Planned Ignoring

Based on the principle of extinction, planned ignoring is very effective in reducing minor disruptive behaviors, especially when the program also involves having students reinforced for appropriate classroom behaviors.

Planned ignoring is, in part, based on the principle of extinction (Nelson & Rutherford, 1983). *Extinction* is defined as stopping the delivery of a reinforcer that has followed a behavior in the past to reduce the likelihood of that behavior being displayed in the future. Planned ignoring involves removing attention contingent on the student's display of a behavior. The underlying reason why this procedure works is that the attention a student receives has been serving as a reinforcer for the student's display of the behavior. Removing the reinforcer should result in a decrease in the disruptive behavior.

Some teachers inadvertently provide students who have been disruptive with extra attention in the form of lectures, scolding, and reprimands following their display of disruptive behaviors. Unfortunately, many students appear to like the added attention, even though the teacher's intent was that the attention be punitive. Teachers often report that they have a student who actually seems to like being yelled at. Observing such a student in the class, it becomes apparent that the student (one of many) is being disruptive to get the added attention.

IMPLEMENTING PLANNED IGNORING

Planned ignoring involves removing the attention (the reinforcer) in a systematic manner. Simply, the teacher does not provide the student with attention when the student is being disruptive. If the teacher can do this in a consistent manner, the disruptive behavior eventually will be reduced to very low rates, if not to zero. The central rule is that, once a behavior is being ignored, the teacher cannot provide the student with attention contingent on the display of that behavior. Obviously, a teacher must ensure that this can be accomplished prior to implementing the program.

IMPORTANT CONSIDERATIONS

Although planned ignoring is often a very useful and effective procedure, some important considerations need to be understood and addressed before it is implemented.

- Initially, after implementing planned ignoring, the student may actually show a brief increase in the behavior. This is called a burst. The teacher must be ready to continue to ignore the disruptive behavior.
- During the burst, the student may also show greater diversity of inappropriate behaviors. Again, the teacher must be ready to ignore these behaviors. If the teacher provides attention to the student at this point in time, the student's display of the disruptive behaviors may actually worsen.
- The target behavior and those that may occur during burst must be behaviors that can be ignored without placing the student or others at risk of being injured. Thus, this procedure is useful mainly for mildly disruptive behaviors. This procedure is not suggested for aggression, or other behaviors that clearly place a person at risk. For example, it would not make sense to ignore a student who is playing with matches. In addition, it would not be appropriate for a teacher to ignore a student who makes such comments like "I'm depressed," "I'm going to kill myself," or any comment that indicates that the student is planning to hurt another person. The teacher should act under the system's regulations and ensure that the student is seen by a pro-

fessional who can assess whether the student is at risk of hurting himself or others.
- If the student has exhibited the disruptive behavior for a long time, and other adults have previously attempted to ignore the behavior, but have failed, the teacher may have greater difficulty using this method. This problem is more pronounced when there has been a mixed history of having the behavior lead to reinforcement for the student. The teacher must take this into consideration prior to using this strategy.
- Planned ignoring is most effective when the student is concurrently receiving reinforcement for an alternative behavior. Thus, it is prudent for a teacher to choose what appropriate behaviors could be reinforced and take the place of the disruptive behavior prior to implementing the program.

Many teachers use planned ignoring on a daily basis. It is common for teachers to say, "If the student is only a little disruptive, I'll ignore him until he calms down." However, it is important for the teacher to ensure that the student will be reinforced while he is cooperative and appropriate, rather than only after he quiets down and "behaves" after being disruptive. Although this procedure is effective, it must be implemented with care and with consideration of the issues just discussed.

16

Time-Out from Positive Reinforcement

> *Time-out, when implemented correctly, is a very effective consequence; however, great emphasis also must be placed on ensuring a positive time-in setting for the students.*

T ime-out refers to placing a student temporarily in a situation that is void of positive reinforcement (Foxx, 1982; Gast & Nelson, 1977a, 1977b). The full name of this procedure is "Time-out From Reinforcement." When a student is placed in time-out, the student should not be in contact with anything that is considered to be positive reinforcement. In a sense, the student is denied contact with anything that is reinforcing or preferred during the brief time-out period.

In contrast to the time-out setting, the "time-in" setting should provide the student with many opportunities to earn positive reinforcement. The time-in setting should be a situation the student wants to be involved in because he or she is able to achieve success and to receive positive reinforcement. The more reinforcing the time-in setting is for a student, the more effective the time-out procedure will be in reducing a negative behavior. The student will be more motivated to remain in the time-in setting and will want to avoid the time-out setting. The student should not be able to have fun or receive unnecessary attention during time-out.

FORMS OF TIME-OUT

If the teacher adheres to the principles of time-out, the actual form of the time-out procedure can be individualized for the students and the classroom. However, a few commonly used versions of time-out have been shown to be effective in an educational setting.

Seclusionary Time-out

Room Time-out

When using this version of time-out, the child is removed from the central classroom area and escorted to a time-out setting. The time-out setting usually is a room located adjacent to the classroom. It should be safe, well-lighted and ventilated, and not frightening. In addition, the area should not contain anything that can be used to have fun such as toys, crayons and paper, or a TV or radio.

Although this version of time-out is often very effective, it has several disadvantages. First, escorting the student to the time-out room must be done quickly. The room must be located close to the location where the student was disruptive. Given the increasing lack of space in schools, placing a student in the time-out room immediately after an incident may not be feasible. Second, if the student is in another room, the teacher will not be able to continue to supervise both the student and the class. Thus, a second person is usually required to ensure that the student in a room time-out is okay. Third, placing a student, especially a relatively young student, in a seclusionary time-out can be very emotionally difficult for the student and may be more punitive than needed to decrease the disruptive behavior. Before implementing a seclusionary time-out procedure, teachers must consult with their administrators to ensure that this form of a consequence is permissible.

Partitioned Area Time-out

Rather than using a separate room, many school systems and teachers prefer to place the student in a partitioned area away from the main activity area in their classroom. Contained in this area may be a chair for the student to sit on while in time-out. This setting should be clearly identified as the "time-out" setting. This version may involve only a chair turned towards the wall or corner and no true partition. If this version is used, the student must not receive any attention from the teacher or other classmates. For example, the student cannot be allowed to turn around and make faces to get laughs from the other students or continually be reminded by the teacher to "face the wall." This added attention is counter to the principle of having the student being removed from positive reinforcement (the attention).

Hall Time-out

Other teachers have used the hallway as a time-out setting. Although this may work with some students, there are some large disadvantages to this approach. First, the teacher assumes that the student will stay and not bolt or escape, which would compound the problem and place the student at risk of getting into more trouble. Second, the student can inadvertently receive reinforcement in the form of added attention from other students, teachers, and administrators while sitting in the hallway. Given these potential problems, this version is not recommended.

Nonseclusionary Time-out

With this approach, the teacher does not remove the student from the classroom area, but instructs the student to place his head down on the desk or temporarily pull his chair back from the group. In other classrooms, teachers remove the materials and their attention for a relatively brief period of time. Furthermore, other teachers will temporarily pause a positive activity, such as stopping a record player, if students are too noisy and wait for a few minutes until they are "under control." This version of time-out is especially useful for mildly disruptive behaviors. Given the relative ease of implementing a nonseclusionary procedure, teachers should consider using this version of time-out prior to using a seclusionary time-out.

Removing the student from the immediate proximity of the other students, but allowing the student to listen and watch the lesson, is sometimes used as a modified version of nonseclusionary time-out. This approach has the advantage that the student does not miss any instruction. However, this approach has the risk of teaching the student to behave appropriately only when he is removed from other students. The teacher must make an effort to teach the student to participate appropriately in group situations. It must be remembered that time-out involves removing the student from reinforcement for only brief periods of time, not on a continued basis.

GENERAL GUIDELINES IN USING TIME-OUT

Although many individuals claim to be using time-out, this procedure often is implemented incorrectly. As with any procedure, time-out must be individualized for the student and implemented by a person who has a firm understanding of the principles that underlie the procedure. In addition, the teacher must be able to evaluate the implementation of the procedure in an objective manner and consult with others prior to using the procedure. Specific guidelines that must be followed to ensure that this procedure is effective, yet not too punishing, include:

- The amount of time a student spends in time-out should be relatively brief. Some professionals suggest a minute for every year of the student's age.
- Although the actual amount of time is relatively brief, a teacher might need to use time-out several times during the initial implementation of the program.
- Prior to using time-out, a teacher should make every effort to increase the likelihood that the student receives positive reinforcement for alternative behaviors. This may preclude the necessity of using time-out.
- The time-out location should pose no threat to the student, nor allow the student to accidently hurt himself or others.
- If a student is placed in time-out for being disruptive to escape or avoid a request, following the time-out period, the student should be re-presented with the request.
- Placing a student in time-out should involve as little physical prompting by the teacher as possible. Although a teacher initially may need to prompt a student to go to time-out,

eventually the teacher should only have to tell the student to "go to time-out, you did _____."
- The teacher should use time-out only for well-defined disruptive behaviors that necessitate its use. If a teacher overuses time-out, the procedure may fail to work.
- After the time-out period has elapsed, the student should rejoin the activity, even if the student is showing some minor disruptive behavior. It might prove beneficial for the teacher to use planned ignoring in relation to the minor disruptive behavior.
- The teacher should not engage the student in a lengthy lecture as to why time-out was used after the student is removed. This may serve as unneeded attention and as a reinforcer. A student might go to time-out just to receive the one-to-one lecture afterwards.
- With many students, the teacher will have the student clean up any mess that was made during time-out afterwards. However, if the teacher feels that this may elevate the level of the problem or provide the student with too much attention, a teacher may decide to not incorporate this component.

If the timeout procedure is effective, the number of times a teacher needs to use it should decrease over time. The disruptive behavior should subside. This is especially true if the teacher places considerable emphasis on incorporating a positive reinforcement component in her class such as a token reinforcement system. As previously indicated, using time-out may provoke more disruptive behavior, and the teacher must decide whether the type and level of disruptive behavior can be handled. If there is any doubt, the teacher should consider implementing a different procedure.

The key is to plan ahead. The teacher should attempt to predict what might happen, and be prepared to implement a backup procedure. By discussing the use of these procedures with supervisors and other relevant individuals, as detailed by the school system's policy, teachers will avoid additional problems and increase the likelihood that the procedures will be effective.

17

Response Cost

> *Related to several other strategies is an intervention known as response cost, which involves having students lose privileges as a result of exhibiting disruptive behaviors.*

PAYING A FINE FOR DISPLAYING DISRUPTIVE BEHAVIOR

Response cost may be seen as a systematic system that involves having a student pay a fine as a result of exhibiting a disruptive act (Foxx, 1982). The amount of loss should be in proportion to the disruptive behavior that was exhibited. Losing a specific amount of reinforcement contingent on the student's display of the disruptive behavior will decrease the probability that the student will display the behavior in the future.

A particularly good example of this procedure was provided to me by a teacher, Miss Reynolds. In her class of third graders, Miss Reynolds had a rule that if a student did not remain on task and complete the assignments in an independent manner, the student had to work on the assignment during free time, rather than going to some of the exciting "centers" that she had set up in her class. The amount of time the student lost was approximately the amount of time the student was off-task. Because the students really enjoyed having time at the centers, Miss Reynolds rarely had to fine a student for not completing his or her work. She further increased the likelihood of the success of her program by incorporating new and exciting centers frequently.

Given the ease of implementing this procedure and the manner in which the punitive level of consequence is in direct relation to the level of disruption, this procedure is used by many teachers. It is convenient and can be used with an individual or a large group of students. Some teachers implement this strategy by giving out small slips of paper that represent so much loss of an activity or other reinforcer. This version is useful if the teacher wants to minimize the attention a student receives from other students for being a "class clown."

USING RESPONSE COST WITH OTHER PROCEDURES

As with many procedures, a response-cost strategy often is combined with other procedures, usually those based on positive reinforcement. Aside from losing reinforcement contingent on the display of disruptive behavior, a student should have many opportunities to earn reinforcement contingent on the display of appropriate behaviors. This can be accomplished using a token program, as described in Chapter 10. For example, if students finish their work early and accurately, they may be given more time to work on other preferred activities or to work at a special center in the classroom.

Aside from combining response cost with positive reinforcement, teachers often use it with other punishment-based contingencies such as time-out. The important rule is to have the rules well defined and the contingencies planned. Other important points to remember in using a response cost procedure include:

1. The student should know the rules ahead of time.
2. The rules should be posted.
3. The teacher needs to use a chart or other clear system of tracking the occurrence of the behavior and the amount of loss.
4. The procedure can be made more effective by incorporating a positive reinforcement component.
5. The criterion for each infraction should be made clear.
6. The teacher needs to consistently enforce the rules and the contingencies for every participating student.

GENERAL CONSIDERATIONS IN USING RESPONSE COST

As with any procedure, some considerations must be dealt with before using a response-cost procedure. Teachers should discuss these considerations with colleagues, administrators, and other significant adults.

- Response-cost procedures may provoke more negative behavior from a student as a result of becoming frustrated for losing too much in a relatively brief period of time. If the negative behaviors are mild, the teacher can use planned ignoring. If they become too severe, then the teacher might need to use a back-up procedure such as time-out. Placing emphasis on reinforcement will help avoid this potential problem.
- If too much emphasis is placed on losing reinforcement for negative behaviors, the teacher inadvertently might begin to pay attention to only negative behaviors in general.
- If a student has already lost all of his reinforcers, such as the amount of time that is available to have "free time," the student may feel he has nothing to lose if he continues to act up. Again, the students must know that the teacher has additional back-up contingencies for such cases.
- If the loss of the reinforcer occurs too long after the occurrence of the behavior, it may be less powerful in teaching the student not to be disruptive. Thus, the loss should occur relatively soon, especially at the start of using this strategy.
- If a student knows that he or she is going to lose a reinforcer during a given session, the student may avoid coming to class. Having a positive reinforcement component will help preclude this possibility.

Response cost is an effective strategy to help a teacher maintain a productive classroom. It gives a teacher a method to teach students that if they exhibit inappropriate disruptive behavior, the system requires that they pay for it by losing some positive reinforcement. They can learn that their own behavior is the reason for either losing or gaining positive reinforcement.

18

Fixing the Environment

There is an old saying, "You break it — you pay for it." In this case, if a student makes a mess, he or she cleans it up.

SETTING THE RULE

This strategy is based on the notion, that if a student's disruptive behavior involves damaging or making a mess, the student should restore the environment. Instead of using this strategy, teachers often use other punishment-based procedures as consequences for such behavior. For instance, if a student throws a book and hits a can of water, the teacher might place the student in a brief time-out. In accordance with "fixing the environment," the student would pick up the book and wipe up the water. Sometimes, a teacher might first place the student in time-out and then have the student fix the environment. Having the student follow through with cleaning up the mess may contribute to the student's understanding that he must be held accountable for his disruptive behavior.

Teachers have reported that this strategy is especially valuable when the student must clean up "his mess" and a little more. For instance, if a student has used a pencil to mark a desk top, the teacher might have the student clean off the entire desk with soap and water, rather than having the student wash only where the mark was made.

If a teacher uses this strategy, the extra work must be reasonable. It would not be reasonable to have a student wash an entire floor, if the student tantrummed and concurrently knocked over his watercolor paints on the floor after being asked to put the paints away. In comparison, having the student clean the mess and put his and several other paint sets away is reasonable. Having the student extend the "cleanup" is referred to as overcorrection or positive practice (see Foxx & Bechtel, 1983).

Another example of using this procedure was reported by an assistant principal who found several youths writing graffiti on a school wall. In discussing this incident with them, the assistant principal discovered that these youths were responsible for much of the graffiti at their school. As part of the consequence, they were given the job of washing several walls that they had marked. This consequence was decided mutually by the school and their parents.

GENERAL CONSIDERATIONS IN USING "FIXING THE ENVIRONMENT"

Before using this procedure, teachers and other professionals should review the following points to ensure that this procedure is appropriate for the student and is implemented correctly.

- The teacher should see the student perform the disruptive act. The teacher should not assume that a particular student was the culprit after hearing a group of students acting up, even if the teacher is told by other students who was to blame. All too often a student becomes the "escape goat" as a result of being disruptive in the past. Common sense is in order.
- The consequence should be fair. The teacher should not use the opportunity to have a student clean up the entire classroom.
- If the student does not follow through with fixing the environment, the teacher should use gentle, but firm prompts to ensure initial cooperation. The prompts used should be the least intrusive prompts possible and should be faded to allow the student to fix the environment in a relatively independent manner.

- If a teacher feels that many physical prompts will be needed to ensure that the student follows through, the teacher should consider using a different approach. The level of prompts that a teacher can implement often is based on school regulations, which the teacher must follow. A teacher should not get rough with a student or get into a physical exchange with a student.
- If a student looks as if he or she is enjoying the clean up activity, the teacher should re-assess the function of the disruptive act. For instance, a teacher of a class of first graders reported that a particular student was disrupting the class by making messes such as knocking books over, spilling water, and writing on the desk. The consequence for such behavior was to have the student clean up the mess with the teacher. When I observed the student in class, it became apparent that the student was making the messes to gain additional attention. From then on, the student was placed in a brief nonseclusionary time-out and was also reinforced for displaying appropriate attention-getting behaviors.
- The cleanup activity should be done soon after the mess is made. If too much time elapses, the relationship between the behavior and the consequence may not be clear to the student.

As with any program, the effects of this strategy must be evaluated systematically. Aside from collecting data on the occurrence of the inappropriate behavior, the teacher should continue efforts to assess why the student is being disruptive from a functional perspective. This may help to pinpoint an appropriate behavior that can be targeted using a positive reinforcement-based program. This approach is commonly used in conjunction with a component that provides positive reinforcement for appropriate classroom behaviors.

PART VII

ASSESSING THE EFFECTIVENESS OF AN INTERVENTION PROGRAM

19

Orientation to Program Assessment

Intervention programs can be further enhanced by assessing their effectiveness in a systematic manner and making changes as needed.

Historically, people have used large group-based designs to determine the effectiveness of intervention programs. However, there are some inherent problems for a teacher in using group-based designs. For example, teachers usually are interested in determining the effects of an intervention program for an individual rather than a group. Furthermore, the averaging of results may hide important negative (or positive) findings that would contraindicate using treatment in certain circumstances. Thus, although group-based designs may be effective in addressing certain experimental questions, their use in applied educational settings may preclude a teacher from concentrating on a specific student and the individual's needs.

Other researchers working in the field of education have proposed the use of the case study approach. A case study is an account of a person in a situation. During the late 19th and early 20th centuries, people were suffering from emotional and behavioral problems. As professionals began to see and treat these individuals, they communicated their clinical judgments and subjective impressions to others using a case-study method. This methodology was one of the most common methodologies used in clinical investigations during the first half of the 20th century. However, there are several problems associated with this approach. For instance, the recording of behavior typically is done in long hand and is very labor intensive. In addition, depending how well the case reports are written, it is very difficult to replicate the findings and thus to be sure that the intervention, per se, was the variable that had an effect on the individual. Often people misjudge the important aspects of the intervention.

Therefore, researchers have developed a methodology that can be used to systematically determine the effectiveness of an intervention program for an individual student. Often referred to as *single case experimental designs,* this approach incorporates principles of group-based designs while placing a substantial emphasis on the individual (Alberto & Troutman, 1990; Barlow & Hersen, 1984; Cooper, Heron, Heward, 1987; Tawney & Gast, 1984). One of the most important principles underlying this approach is the need to identify whether there is a cause and effect between introducing an intervention and producing a positive change in the student's behavior. Although books have been written on this topic, this section centers on aspects of this approach that teachers have found interesting and useful in educational settings.

ASSESSING THE LEVEL OF THE BEHAVIOR BEFORE INTERVENTION

The purpose of using single-case experimental designs is to find out whether the behavior of a student will be changed as a result of introducing a particular intervention. In modifying a behavior, one of the first steps is to obtain a record of its level prior to intervention. This level of the behavior is the *baseline.* During the baseline period, the student's behavior is observed over several instances to clearly define the level of behavior. In addition, by gathering data over several instances, a teacher can determine whether there is variability in the student's display of the behavior due to specific antecedents, consequences, or other variables.

The length of a baseline phase can vary substantially, but usually requires a minimum of three to five sessions. During this phase, the teacher needs to determine if there is a trend in the data (descending, ascending). If a student's display of a disruptive behavior is decreasing during baseline, the teacher will not be able to determine if the intervention procedures have an effect. Although the decrease is "good," unfortunately the teacher will not be able to determine why the decrease occurred and will not be able to implement a treatment program in the future if the behavior spontaneously reappears. Thus, it is important that a baseline phase be continued until the trend is either stable or is moving in the direction opposite to that desired.

A word of caution is in order. Although it is important to establish baseline levels for disruptive behaviors, teachers must consider several other factors when deciding the length of the baseline. If a student loses his or her educational placement due to a continued display of aggression, taking a lengthy baseline may be counterproductive. In addition, it may be too taxing on a teacher or teaching assistant to record several observations prior to intervention. During the baseline phase, the teacher must remember why it is necessary to collect data. The data collected during baseline will be compared to data collected subsequently to determine the effectiveness of the intervention program and to make modifications as needed.

DISPLAYING THE BASELINE DATA

Although there are many methods of displaying baseline data, teachers typically use a set of axes referred to as the ordinate and abscissa. The vertical axis (up and down) is the ordinate, and the horizontal axis (left to right) is the abscissa. The ordinate is used to note the quantity or rate of a behavior while the abscissa is used to express time, such as sessions or days. Figure 19–1 shows data collected using a frequency measurement system on the number of disruptive acts shown during a 2½ hour morning kindergarten class. The child, as can be seen, exhibited between three and five disruptive acts per day. More importantly, these data show that the level of disruptions was stable. Rather than waiting for additional data to be collected, the teacher of this child introduced a treatment the next day.

A second example is presented in Figure 19–2. These data are from a teacher who was interested in decreasing the amount of time a second grade student dawdled before beginning independent assignments. The teacher recorded the amount of time be-

Mike's Disruptive Behaviors

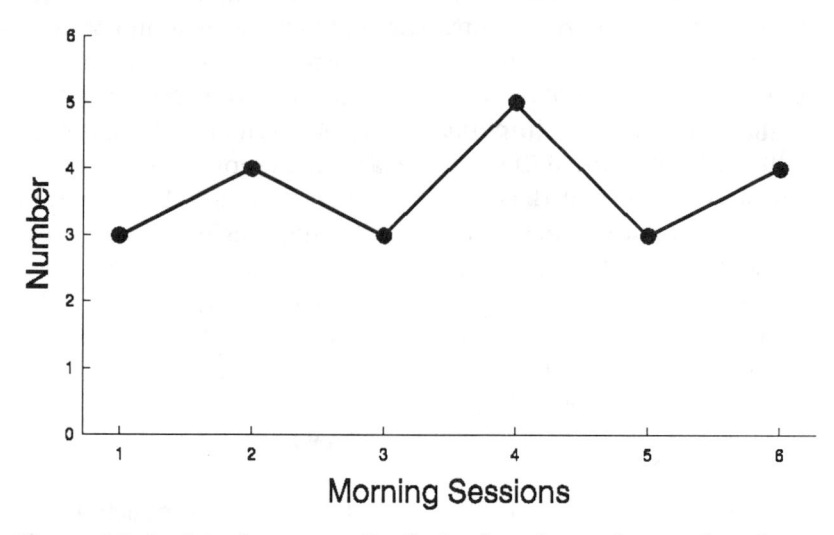

Figure 19-1. *A teacher can easily display how frequently a student shows disruptive behaviors. This figure shows the number of disruptive behaviors that Mike, a kindergarten student, exhibited during each morning session.*

Larry's Dawdling Behaviors

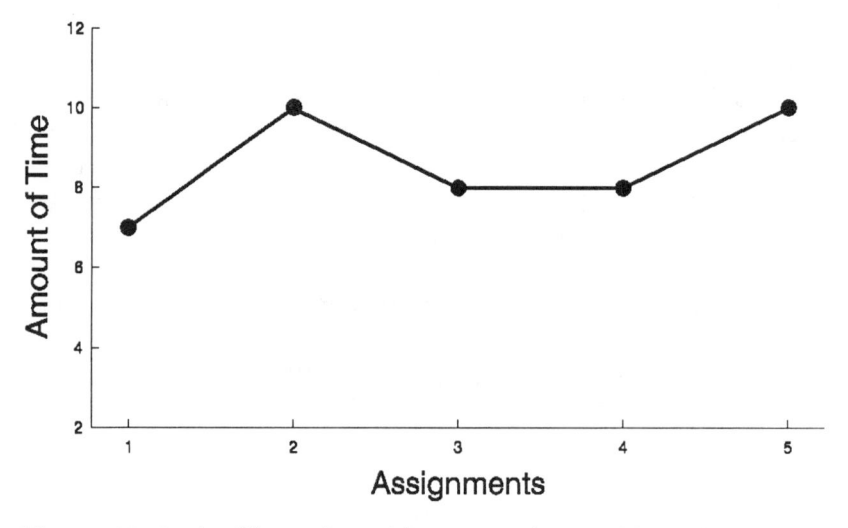

Figure 19-2. *An illustration of how a teacher could graph response latency data.*

tween the end of the instruction and the point in time the student started the assignment. As can be seen in Figure 19-2, the student took approximately 7 to 10 minutes to begin his assignments. During this time, he was observed to sharpen his pencil repeatedly, clean off his desk, and straighten his books. Although each of these behaviors may be important, this student performed these behaviors throughout the day after the teacher provided an assignment. The excessive display of these behaviors interfered with his efforts to initiate and complete his independent assignments.

20

Program Assessment Strategies

Assessing the effects of an intervention program in a systematic manner helps teachers to document their efforts in decreasing classroom behavior problems.

Borrowing from the systematic methodology employed by applied behavior analysts, several methods of assessing the direct effects of intervention programs are described in this chapter (Barlow & Hersen, 1984; Tawney & Gast, 1984). Although some of the assessment designs appear complicated, teachers and other professionals have found them to have great utility. The main reason to use a design is to allow a teacher to systematically determine whether an intervention is influencing the target behavior.

THE A-B COMPARISON

A simple A-B design is presented in Figure 20–1. The A condition is usually a pretreatment assessment or baseline of a behavior that is behavioral defined. This behavior is measured at length to demonstrate its stability before treatment is introduced. When the teacher sees some stability, treatment is initiated and administered in the B condition until a criteria or goal set by the teacher has been met.

A-B Graph

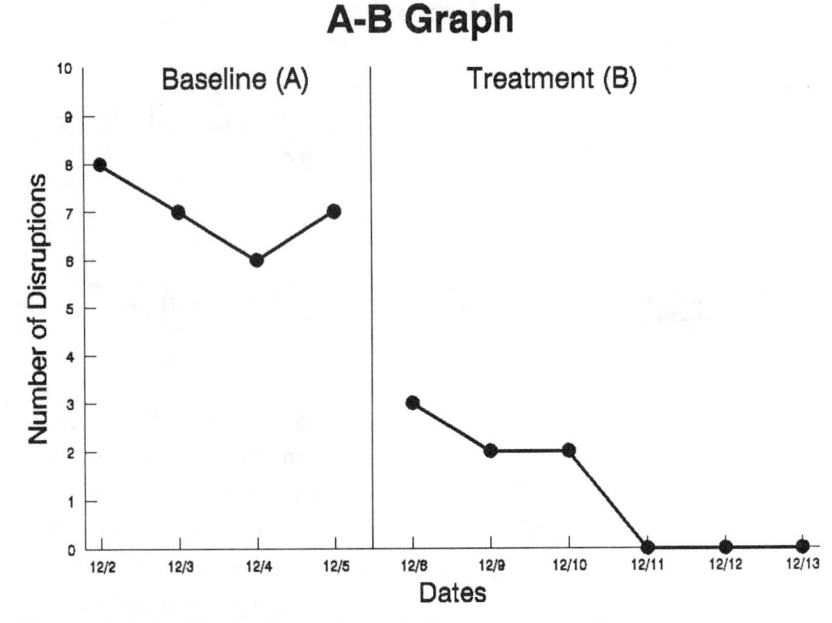

Figure 20–1. *Illustration of an A-B comparison design.*

The A-B design has several strengths, including its ease of implementation. However, sometimes it is difficult to know for sure whether the change in the behavior was a result of intervention or due to other events that were occurring in the student's life at the same time. For example, a teacher established a program to facilitate greater communication skills for a student. However, at approximately the same time the teacher started the program, the parents started the child at a private speech therapist. Although the teacher was convinced that the school program was producing the changes seen in the student, the parents argued that the speech therapist was the basis of the student's gains.

Because resources are not endless, intervention programs must be evaluated for their utility. In this case, if the teacher's program was responsible for producing the change, the parents could have saved a considerable amount of money and time. If, on the other hand, the private speech therapist was having the effect with the student, the intervention program could have been "transferred" to the school. Unfortunately, an A-B design does not always allow a person to know whether other variables that were introduced at the same time contributed to the change in the student's behavior.

THE MULTIPLE-BASELINE DESIGN

Given the uncertainty of attributing the change in a student's behavior to the intervention program when an A-B design is used, professionals have turned to using a design known as a multiple-baseline design. In a multiple-baseline design, treatment is introduced at different times to determine its effects on two or more classes of behavioral observations (Baer, Wolf, & Risley, 1968). There are many different kinds of multiple-baseline designs including:

- A multiple-baseline design across *behaviors*
- A multiple-baseline design across *students*
- A multiple-baseline design across *settings*

Let us discuss each major version of the multiple-baseline design in relation to various variables and as to why this is a valid design. In contrast to the A-B design, in a multiple-baseline design, control comes from a replication of treatment effects. As described below, replication can be done across behaviors, students, and settings.

Multiple-Baseline Design Across Behaviors

In a multiple-baseline design across behaviors, the purpose is to determine if a single treatment is effective in changing two or more behaviors in the same way for a particular student. The behaviors selected for treatment need to be different enough from one another that treatment of one does not influence the other until it receives treatment. On the other hand, the behaviors cannot be so different that a single treatment is inapplicable to them.

The same treatment is applied to all selected behaviors, but it is administered to the behaviors in a sequence. A multiple baseline design across two behaviors is illustrated in Figure 20–2. Initially, a baseline measurement is taken for both behaviors. When stability is reached on the two behaviors, treatment is started on the first one. The second behavior continues in baseline while the first is treated. When treatment of the first behavior is completed, or at least is being clearly influenced by treatment, treatment is also introduced to the second behavior until a behavior change is demonstrated.

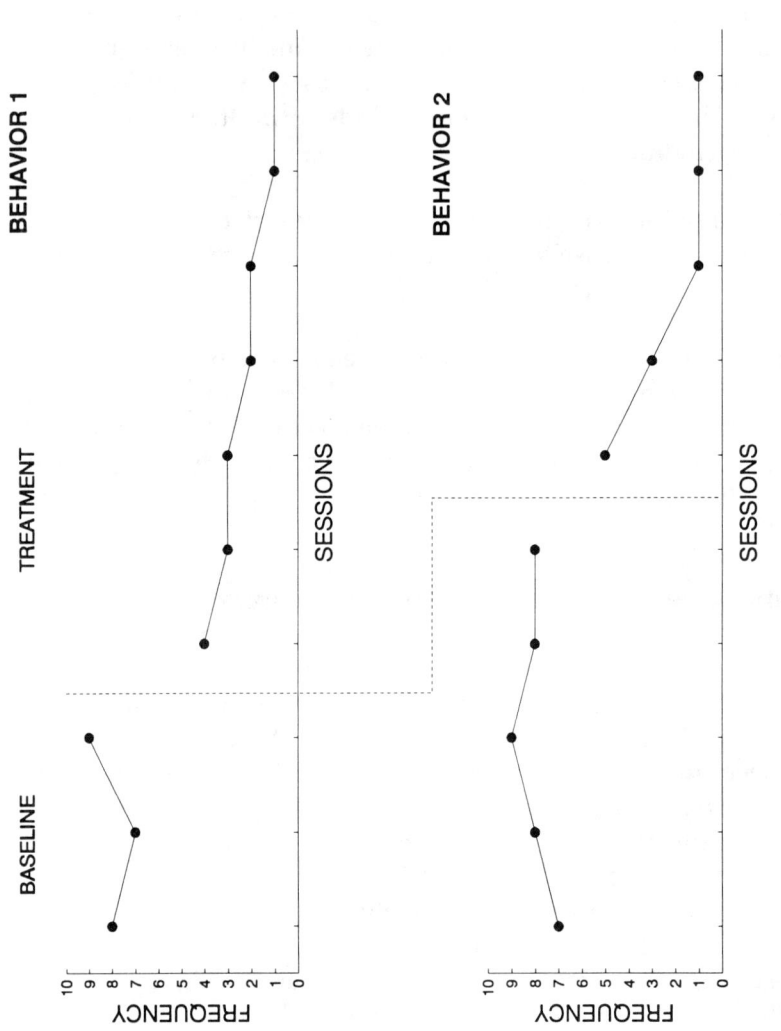

Figure 20–2. *Illustration of a multiple-baseline design across two behaviors.*

In a multiple-baseline design across behaviors, it is assumed that the second behavior will continue to show stability in the protracted baseline until treatment for the first behavior is terminated. It is the second behavior that brings the experimental control in a multiple-baseline design across behaviors. If the second behavior does not change while the first is in treatment, this stability demonstrates that the intervention (known as the independent variable) affects only the behavior (known as the dependent variable) that was directly targeted. The stable baseline of the second (untreated) behavior also demonstrates that time, maturation, and other extraneous variables are not changing the behavior, rather than the intervention. If these variables influenced the first behavior, they would also operate on the second behavior, and the second behavior would change prior to the introduction of treatment. To ensure that the treatment program is the reason why there was a change in the first behavior, application of the treatment to the second behavior must result in a similar change. To be very certain, some professionals suggest that a multiple baseline design involve applying the intervention sequentially to three to four different behaviors.

For example, Mr. Bill, a teacher of a group of middle school age students with behavioral disorders,was interested in reducing several disruptive behaviors with a student named Mark. His disruptive behaviors included loud talking, slamming books on the desk, and throwing paper basketballs into the trashcan from his desk. Based on the A-B-C data he collected, Mr. Bill saw that Mark typically did these behaviors for no apparent reason. Sometimes it appeared that he did them for attention, other times to get out of work, and other times it was just uncertain. Rather than waiting for it to become clear why Mark was being disruptive, Mr. Bill wanted to introduce an intervention program.

After discussing Mark with his previous teacher, Mr. Bill discovered that Mark had a long history of being disruptive. Furthermore, several previous attempts to reduce Mark's disruptive behaviors had failed. Previous attempts had involved targeting all of the disruptive behaviors at once with a response-cost component. This resulted in Mark becoming physically agitated. I suggested if Mr. Bill wanted to intervene with a response-cost component, he should introduce it on a single behavior at a time in accordance with a multiple-baseline design.

Specifically, my suggestions for Mr. Bill included that he first begin his intervention by setting up a token economy system based on positive reinforcement to provide Mark with tokens, social praise, and an opportunity to purchase back-up reinforcers. If the three disruptive behaviors were not reduced, Mr. Bill could introduce the second component which entailed having a response-cost procedure in place for the three behaviors. However, given Mark's previous history of becoming physically agitated if too many rules were changed at once, Mr. Bill could introduce the response cost in accordance with a multiple-baseline design across the three disruptive behaviors. This is illustrated in Figure 20-3.

After collecting some data during the baseline condition, Mr. Bill would first introduce the response-cost procedure for loud talking. After seeing a reduction in Mark's loud talking, Mr. Bill could begin to target the next behavior of slamming books down on the table. Again, after observing a reduction in this behavior, Mr. Bill could then target the last behavior, which involved throwing paper basketballs. Using the multiple-baseline design across behaviors would allow Mr. Bill to monitor each behavior and to assess the effects of the response-cost component of his intervention program. Implementation of the token economy reinforcement program would allow Mark to gain access to many preferred activities, which might include a weekly game of one-on-one basketball with Mr. Bill.

Multiple-Baseline Design Across Students

In a multiple-baseline design across students, a particular treatment is applied sequentially across students. In contrast to the multiple-baseline design across behaviors, this design requires that the treatment is introduced across students on the same behavior. The purpose of using this design is to document that an intervention program can be used effectively with more than a single student. Typically, this design is used with students who are similar to each other in terms of age, level of functioning, communication skills, or other pertinent child characteristics. Using similar students increases the likelihood that a single intervention program will be effective. If a teacher has students who are quite diverse, the teacher should note how the students vary across such variables as those previously noted, in case the intervention program is not equally effective for each student.

PROGRAM ASSESSMENT STRATEGIES ≡ **159**

Multiple Baseline Across Behaviors

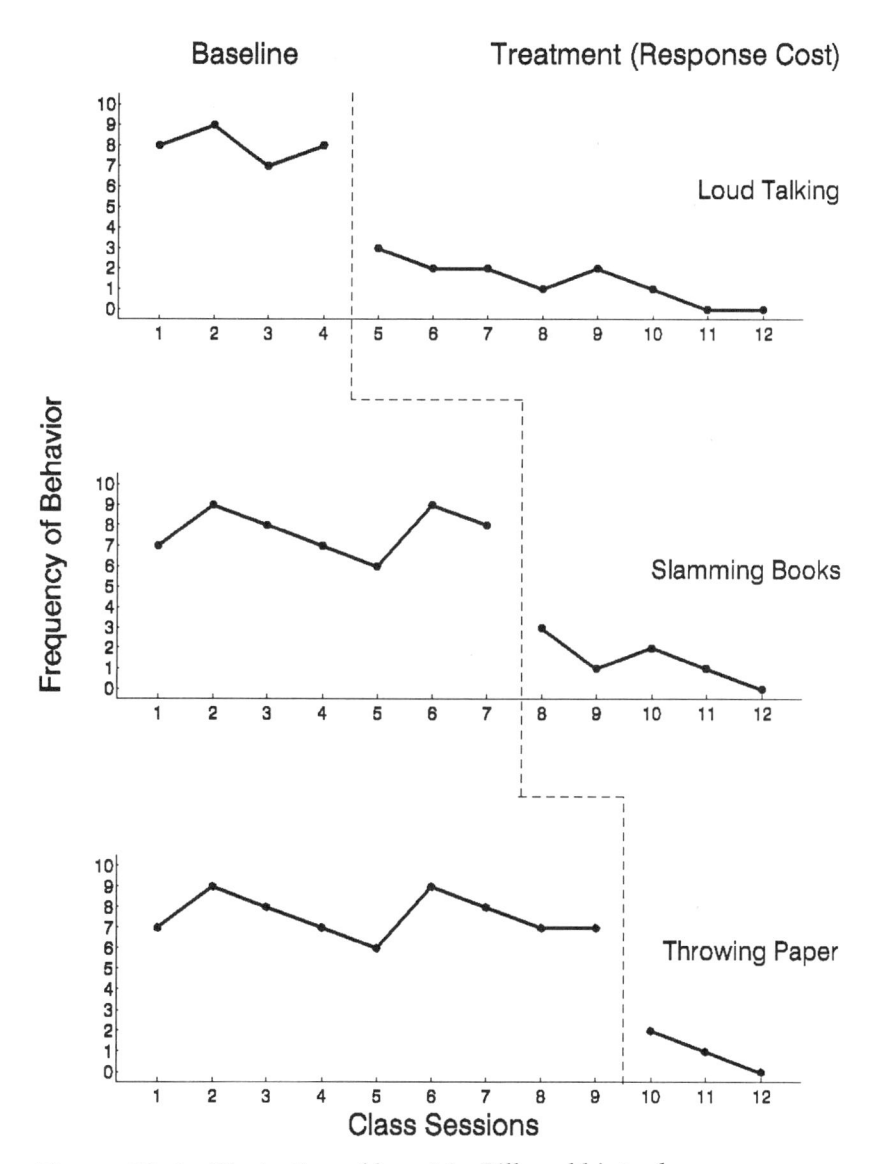

Figure 20-3. *Illustration of how Mr. Bill could introduce a response-cost procedure sequentially across three disruptive behaviors displayed by Mark.*

Multiple-Baseline Design Across Settings

A multiple-baseline design across settings can be used to assess whether a treatment is effective in more than one setting for a given student. The principles remain the same in all multiple-baseline designs. In this design, baseline data must be taken across all settings and the treatment is then introduced sequentially in each setting. A multiple-baseline design across settings could be used to assess the effects of a response-cost procedure on a student's disruptive behavior (see Figure 20–4). Baseline data on the child's disruptions would be taken concurrently across settings. The intervention would then be introduced, for example, in the student's homeroom class. After it was shown to be effective, the intervention would be introduced sequentially across the student's English and math classes after the protracted baselines.

Multiple-Baseline (Probe) Design

At times, baselines for untreated behaviors are obtained intermittently, perhaps in every third or fourth training session for the treated behavior (Horner & Baer, 1978). Intermittent measures are less efficient in complying with the demands of a multiple-baseline design, but they are more practical when lengthy baselines are required. This variation is referred to as a multiple-baseline probe design.

THE A-B-A-B DESIGNS

The A-B-A-B Design

The A-B-A-B design is one of the simplest strategies used to assess the effects of an intervention on a target behavior (Baer, Wolf, & Risley, 1968). As shown in Figure 20–5, in an A-B-A-B design the teacher collects baseline data in the A condition. Next, the teacher introduces the intervention during the B treatment condition. Subsequently, the teacher (briefly) withdraws the intervention and returns to the A condition to ensure that the intervention was

Multiple Baseline Across Settings

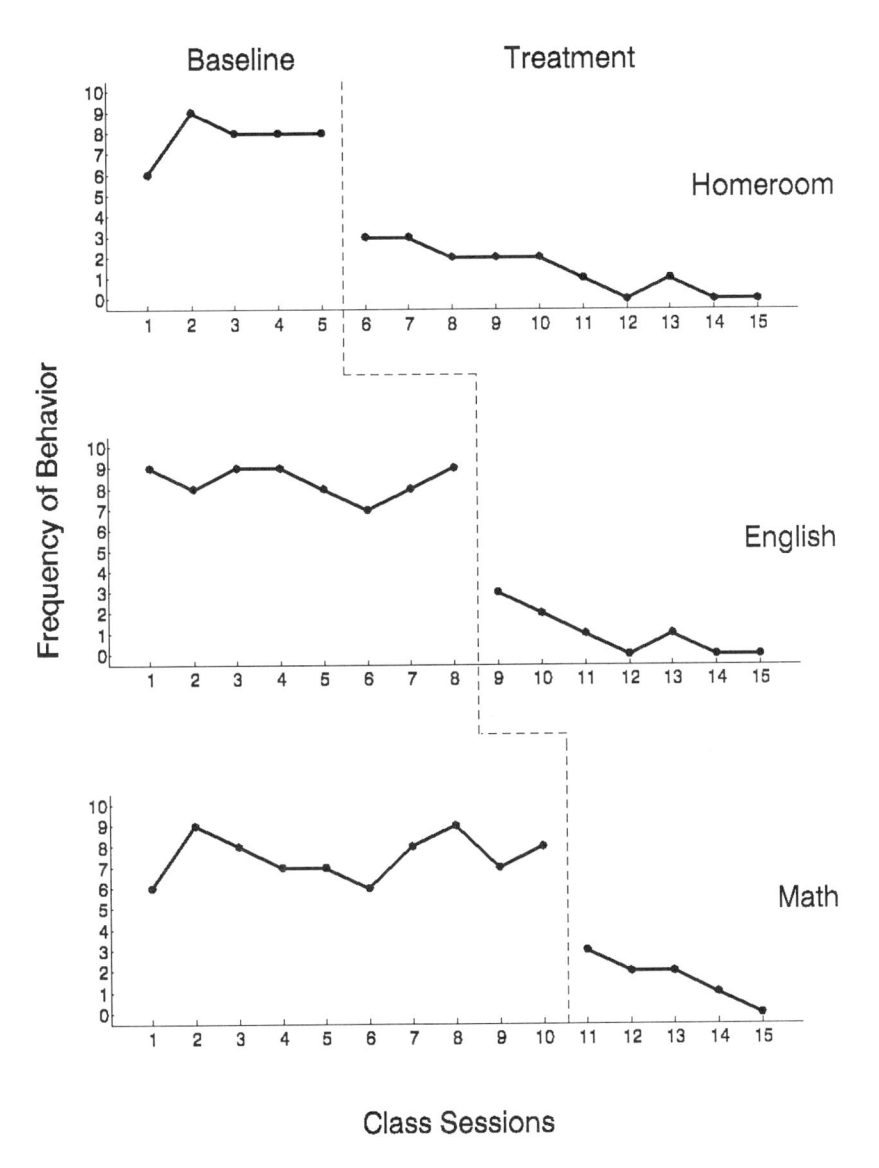

Figure 20-4. *Illustration of how a multiple-baseline design could be used to introduce an intervention program sequentially across three settings for a single student.*

A-B-A-B Reversal Design

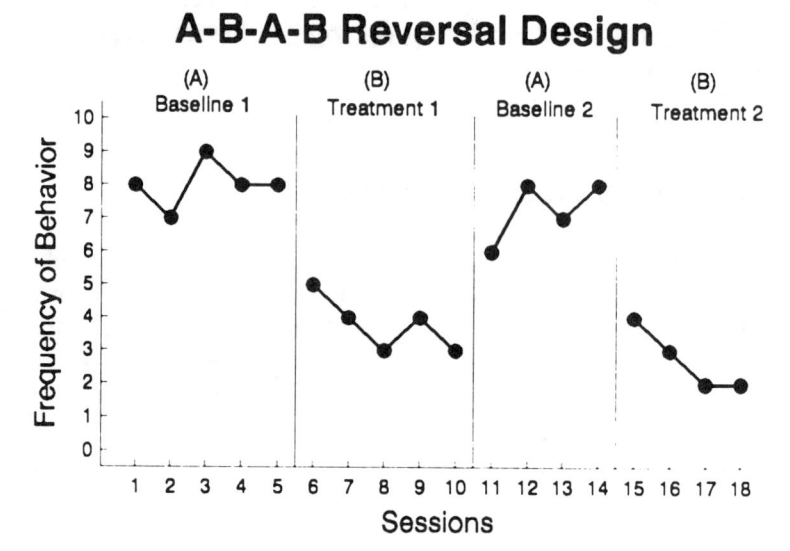

Figure 20-5. *An illustration of an A-B-A-B design.*

the variable that produced the increase. During the second A condition, the behavior should return to approximately baseline levels, or at least head in that direction. Lastly, following the second A condition, the teacher reintroduces the intervention program to make sure it has the same effect on the target behavior.

There are some problems inherent in this design. First, the teacher might decide that it would not be advantageous to withdraw the intervention. For some students with certain behaviors, it would not be wise to withdraw the intervention. Second, this design assumes that the behavior can reverse. Some behaviors or skills may not reverse. Again, this must be taken into consideration prior to using this design.

The A-B-C-B-C Design

After introducing the treatment in the B condition, a teacher realizes that the intervention is having little effect. Rather than giving up and trying something different, the teacher decides to modify the intervention and keep track of its effects as denoted as the C condition. If intervention during the C condition has an effect, the teacher can ensure that the intervention produced the effect by briefly going back to the B condition. If the behavior reverses, the teacher can reintroduce the C condition to replicate the effects of the intervention program.

THE CHANGING CRITERION DESIGN

The changing criterion design is a variation of the multiple-baseline design that can be used to evaluate the effects of an intervention on a single, gradually acquired (complex) behavior (Hartman & Hall, 1976). It is especially appropriate for studying the effectiveness of shaping procedures. There are two primary phases in a changing criterion design: a baseline and a treatment phase. During baseline, a single behavior is monitored over time until a stable response is achieved. Baseline performance is subsequently used to establish an initial criterion level, and treatment is then introduced. Once the initial criterion is reached, a more stringent criterion is established. This is repeated until a terminal level is reached.

With the changing criterion design, experimental control is demonstrated when the change in the target behavior closely corresponds to and stabilizes at each new criterion level. Stable responding at each new criterion level provides a baseline for successive treatment phases. The co-occurrence of change in the behavior and shift in criterion levels during each treatment phase provides within-subject replication of the experimental effect. Thus, the control elements previously discussed for multiple-baseline design, stable base rate and replication, are also evident in the changing criterion design.

THE ALTERNATING TREATMENT DESIGN

As its name implies, the basic strategy in this design is the rapid alternation of two or more treatments or conditions for a particular student (Barlow & Hayes, 1979). Rapid does not imply every hour or day; typically, it implies every time the student is seen. If a student is seen once a week, the treatment is changed every week, either being a treatment A or a treatment B. The order should be done in a relatively random manner. Typically, in using this design, three phases exist:

1. Baseline phase
2. Experimental treatment phase
3. Application phase

Because this design can be used to compare more than one intervention simultaneously, it may enable a teacher to formulate a treatment plan much quicker. This design can be used when the behavior that is targeted is irreversible or when a reversal is undesirable. Furthermore, because the conditions are alternated very rapidly, it takes less time to assess the effectiveness of the intervention. Lastly, if a no-treatment condition is used during the second phase, a lengthy baseline is not required. One problem associated with this design is that one intervention may interfere with the effects of a second intervention. This is referred to as multiple-treatment interference or carryover effects.

PART VIII

INTEGRATING A BEHAVIOR MANAGEMENT PROGRAM INTO A STUDENT'S INDIVIDUALIZED EDUCATIONAL PROGRAM

21

Strategies for Designing and Implementing Successful Programs

Teaching appropriate and productive classroom behaviors and reducing behavior problems should be considered as important as teaching math, science, writing, or any other topic.

Teaching appropriate and productive classroom behaviors and reducing behavior problems should be considered as important for some students as teaching math, science, writing, or any other classroom topic. For students who have a history of being disruptive, teaching such skills is imperative. Unfortunately, in some schools, the approach that is taken is to wait until a student misbehaves and then to implement a punishment-based intervention program.

Rather than acting reactively, many professionals argue that school professionals must act proactively (Rosenberg & Burke, 1992). That is, a plan must be developed and in place to help these students learn more appropriate productive classroom and social skills. A proactive plan reduces disruptive classroom behaviors and minimizes the need for teachers to implement a punishment-based program.

For example, a teacher in an inner city school used a proactive program to teach her students efficient study skills. She reported that since she began to teach study skills, her students typically remained on task longer, scored higher on class tests, and appeared more motivated. The time she spent teaching the students efficient study skills was well spent.

Recently, greater emphasis has been placed on proactively teaching productive social skills to students with behavior disorders, rather than acting only reactively by punishing them for being disruptive or aggressive. The students are taught positive social skills for dealing with situations that previously would have provoked disruptive behavior. Some schools have given social skills training equal status with teaching math, reading, or any other subject area. The amount of effort taken to ensure that students learn appropriate classroom and social skills serves as an investment in the student's future.

DESIGNING INDIVIDUALIZED PROGRAMS

Students are individuals and the manner in which teachers approach their behavior problems also needs to be individualized. All too often, however, I have seen professionals who specialize in behavior management who use one or two methods to deal with disruptive behaviors exhibited by students, regardless of their ages and levels of functioning. The treatment plan is given to the teacher in the form of a written "protocol," which states a sequence of activities that must be followed to ensure that a student's disruptive behavior will be decreased. No changes are permissible. One protocol fits all.

If there is one lesson that I have learned (although I have learned more) from working with students, teachers, and school administrators, it is that students are individuals and the manner in which we approach them and their disruptive behaviors must be determined by factors associated with each student. Specifically, an intervention program must be individualized in three ways:

1. *The program must meet the student's individualized needs.* As in any topic of study, behavior management programs must be designed and implemented to meet the individual needs of a student. Even though a program, such as a token program, can be implemented with a large number of students, the program should be flexible enough for a teacher to individualize it for each student. A teacher of math or reading has the flexibility to approach the students of a large class in a manner that promotes individualization of work. Similarly, teachers should be given the resources to allow them to individualize their efforts to teach productive classroom and social skills.

2. *The program must be individualized for the teacher.* Many years ago, the number of approaches that a teacher could choose from was relatively small. Today, we often have many options and several refined programs that have an equal likelihood of being successful. Rather than "telling" teachers what specific programs must be implemented, it is more advantageous to have the consultant and the teacher work together to individualize the program for the teacher. All teachers do not teach the same, and we should not expect them all to implement exactly the same behavior management program when there are alternatives that are equally effective and acceptable to the system.

3. *Programs should be individualized for the classroom.* A classroom is a combination of a specific group of students, a teacher (and an instructional assistant), and the physical arrangement of furniture and materials. Although similar, there are some differences in classrooms, and these must be taken into consideration while forming an intervention program. For example, a professional colleague of mine could not understand why a teacher was against introducing a program that would have required the teacher to spend a considerable amount of one-to-one time with the student who was exhibiting tantrums. The student was one of 15 students in a class with no teaching assistant. I suggested that an alternative intervention program be designed while keeping the teacher-student ratio in mind.

WRITING SHORT- AND LONG-TERM BEHAVIORAL OBJECTIVES

"If it is worth doing, it is worth doing right." Doing it right means, in part, being organized. A teacher can help ensure success by writing behavioral objectives for a student who has a history of being disruptive. In many school systems, teachers automatically include a behavior management component in a student's Individualized Educational Plan (IEP). If a student is in a regular education classroom, many teachers still find it very useful to write behavioral objectives as part of the intervention process. If a teacher follows a few rules, writing behavioral objectives can be accomplished with relative ease.

Short-Term Behavioral Objectives

A behavioral objective is a clearly written statement that states a proposed criterion-based change in a student's behavior. The following are examples of behavioral objectives in relation to teaching students appropriate classroom skills.

> Bill will complete 100% of his assigned math sheet during the 20-minute independent practice period.
>
> Mary will remain in her seat throughout the morning, unless she raises her hand and receives permission to get up.
>
> John will initiate interactions with other students by first addressing them by their names during 80% of the occasions that occur during the afternoon session.
>
> Joshua will begin to comply within one minute after a request is presented 18 out of 20 occasions.
>
> Following the completion of a row of six math problems, Mark will self-record his completion by marking an "X" on the self-monitoring card.

A behavioral objective serves as a basis for evaluating the success of an intervention program that is implemented to change the behavior of a student. It also serves as a way to communicate to other adults exactly what the focus of the intervention is for a student and clearly sets the criterion for success. As can be seen in the examples of behavioral objectives just given, three essential components must be included.

State Who Will Be Involved

The behavioral objective must state who will be involved. The who typically is a single student; however, it can also refer to a group of students or to an entire class. For instance, the following three behavioral objectives were written for a group of students.

The students in reading Group A will come in from recess and within three minutes they will start completing their assignment for four out of five days in the week.

All of the members of the class will whisper during the 30-minute library session.

One hundred percent of the students in Mrs. Lion's class will walk single file down the hall from their room to the cafeteria each day of the week.

Clearly Define the Target Behavior

A behavioral objective must clearly define the target behavior that will be done by the student(s). Typically, the behavior is operationally defined and should meet three criteria:

- *Objectivity*. The definition should refer to observable characteristics of the behavior or environment. Definitions should not refer to inferred thoughts, feelings, or other inner states.
- *Clarity*. The definition should not be ambiguous. After reading the definition, two or more observers should be able to record the target behavior in a reliable manner.
- *Completeness*. Ideally, the definition should delineate the boundaries of the target behavior.

Examples of target behaviors are as follows:

_____ will sit in his chair with both feet on the ground.

_____ will complete every math problem on his sheet in a correct manner.

_____ will record each occurrence of an appropriate social initiation.

_____ will raise her hand when she has a question and will wait to be called upon.

_____ will walk to the cafeteria behind the line leader.

In addition to the actual behavior, some professionals suggest including additional information about the context or setting in which the student will perform the behavior, the type of instructions given, and the materials that will be used. As long as such information can be included in a concise manner and contributes to a clearly written objective, it is wise to include some of this information.

The Acceptable Criterion

Each behavioral objective should state the criterion that will be used to determine whether the program is successful in changing the student's behavior. The criterion should be stated in a manner that allows empirical assessment. For instance, a criterion could include:

1. The percentage of requests complied with by a student
2. The number of problems completed correctly on a math sheet
3. The length of time the student takes to initiate a response to an instruction presented by a teacher
4. The amount of time a student remains on-task during a 30-minute session
5. The number of activities the group completes

The criterion chosen should be based on the needs of the particular student, the level of proficiency of other students who typically exhibit the target behavior, and any other particulars of the situation. If a teacher has an ultimate criterion of 100%, the teacher should consider lowering the criterion during the initial portion of the intervention to help a student meet success.

Long-Term Behavioral Objectives

A behavioral objective can be written to involve a student in mastering a simple target behavior, a relatively complex task, or an advanced skill. A relatively simple target behavior might involve teaching a student to complete assignment sheets with a one-to-one assistant. A more advanced target behavior might involve having the student learn to complete an assignment independently. The second objective is based on the notion that the student can complete the assignment if an assistant is present. A teacher could write the second, more long-term, objective for the student when writing the first objective.

As in this example, long-term objectives are often extensions of the short-term objectives and are based on the student's acquisition of them. They are written in the same manner, except sometimes a teacher will include a phrase such as, "After the student meets the criteria for (Behavior A), then the student will . . . " A series of objectives helps to communicate to others the planned course of action for a student over an extended period of time. In addition, having long-term goals helps teachers put what they are teaching the students on a daily basis into perspective in terms of the student's long-term development.

It is often advantageous for teachers to build alternatives into the program. Not having preplanned alternatives, often leads to programs that become less effective for the student and waste valuable teaching time. For instance, on many occasions, I have been asked to consult with teachers who are working with students with pervasive developmental disorders. These students commonly have severe difficulty communicating with others using a verbal communication system, and their communication difficulties result in disruptive behaviors. The typical question asked is whether a program should target teaching the student to use speech versus some other communication system to reduce the disruptive behaviors. The decision of whether to teach a student speech versus some other communication system, such as sign language, depends on several factors, including the age and level of functioning of the student and the success of previous attempts to teach the student to use speech.

Unfortunately, teachers often choose an approach or goal that is overly narrow, and when success does not occur, they continue to try to attain the goal over an extended period of time. By continuing an unsuccessful approach, the student fails to make progress in acquiring any functional communication system. Building some flexibility into a program allows teachers the opportunity to continue their efforts of teaching students to communicate even if they fail with one method and need to switch to another mode of communication. In defining alternative target behaviors, teachers must consider input from a number of sources including other school personnel and the parents of the students.

ASSESSING AND PROGRAMMING FOR GENERALIZING AND MAINTENANCE

Planning for and assessing generalization of educational and treatment gains is vital. Many years ago, professionals simply assumed that generalization occurred naturally and easily for all students. Today, we know that for some students generalization is an exception and not the rule. Lack of generalizaton is one of the most common and difficult problems faced by educators.

Defining Generalization

In discussing generalization, it is first important to provide a definition. One of the most common definitions seen in the literature is from Stokes and Baer (1977).

> Generalization will be considered to be the occurrence of relevent behavior under different, non-training conditions (i.e., across subjects, settings, people, behaviors, and/or time) without the scheduling of the same events in those conditions as had been scheduled in the training conditions. (p. 350)

From a teacher's perspective, generalization may be viewed as occurring in the following fashion:

- *Generalization across students.* After teaching one student a new skill, other students begin to demonstrate increases in that skill. For example, after reinforcing a student for being in his seat, the teacher notices that other students remain in their seats more often (possibly from observing the student receiving reinforcement).
- *Generalization across settings.* A student transfers the treatment gains from one setting to another while he is with the same teacher. For example, after a student was taught to remain in his seat in his class, the student also began

to stay seated while eating his lunch in the cafeteria when his teacher was present.
- *Generalizaton across people.* A student shows similar gains while interacting with people who were not involved in implementing the program such as other teachers, parents, or classmates. For example, a student who was taught improved social skills might begin to use them while interacting with others.
- *Generalization across time.* The student retains the use of newly acquired skills over time. For example, even though the teacher faded a token reinforcement program for a student, the student maintained high levels of productive classroom skills.
- *Generalization across tasks.* The student uses the target behavior while working on a different task. For example, after teaching a student to monitor his on-task behavior in math, he uses the self-monitoring program to monitor his on-task behavior in reading.

Being aware of the difficulties such students have in generalizing their gains, in itself, can help. If a teacher monitors for generalization, but it does not occur, the teacher can alter the intervention program. For example, if a student does not show a reduction in his disruptive behaviors in other classrooms after he clearly has shown a decrease in his homeroom, the teacher can transfer the program to the other settings by training the other teachers to implement the behavior management program. Although this is not true generalization, it is an effective strategy to promote transfer. If the teacher does not assess for generalization, a student may continue to exhibit disruptive behaviors in the other settings. Given how busy teachers are, there is no reason why a teacher needs to re-invent the wheel. Sharing effective programs helps the students as well as busy colleagues.

Generalization Promotion Techniques

Teachers need a systematic plan to ensure that the gains seen in the classroom will transfer to other school, home, and community settings. Furthermore, teachers should actively facilitate the transfer of gains achieved in their classrooms to other teachers' classrooms in the following year. Although generalization remains one of the most difficult problems for teachers and other professionals, researchers have begun to develop general strategies that can be used to facilitate generalization (Horner, Dunlap, & Koegel, 1988). It is beyond the scope of this section to discuss these procedures in depth, but a brief presentation follows. For a more thorough presentation of these strategies, please refer to the respective references.

Sequential Modification

Sequential modification is a strategy that involves targeting a behavior across several settings in a sequential manner until the student begins to demonstrate generalization to nontreatment settings. For example, Mr. Richards was working with an 18-year-old student with severe retardation who had a history of being disruptive during meals. On numerous occasions he observed the student (Chris) throwing his food on the floor. When he brought this concern to the attention of Chris's parents, they reported that he frequently threw his food on the floor at home, especially near the end of the meals. Mr. Richards asked the parents to collect some A–B–C data at home, as he was doing in the school cafeteria. After reviewing the data collected over several days, Mr. Richards began to see a pattern. It appeared that Chris was throwing his food on the ground after he had eaten a fairly large quantity. In terms of consequences, most often, Chris was allowed to leave or was asked to pick up the food and then asked to leave. On those occasions when Chris was asked to pick up the food, he did so without an argument.

Based on these data, and reports from other adults, Mr. Richards concluded that Chris might be throwing his food to signal others that he was finished eating and wanted to leave. Mr. Richards and the parents agreed that it would be nice to eliminate this disruptive behavior. The parents had stopped taking Chris to public restaurants as a result of this problem. Mr. Richards and the parents established an intervention program that involved teaching Chris to appropriately signal others when he was done eating, rather than throwing his food.

After several days of working on this skill in the school cafeteria, Chris started to reliably use this appropriate signal. Mr. Richards began to reinforce Chris's use of this signal during class outings to a fast food restaurant. Next, the parents began to work on this target behavior at home. After a few meals, Chris began to use the signal in a highly reliable manner. Without having to continue to work directly on this target behavior, Chris began to also use this signal while he was with his parents or Mr. Richards in other, nontreatment settings. Of course, both Mr. Richards and the parents provided Chris with praise. However, they did not have to prompt Chris to use it, as they had in the first three settings. Thus, after teaching Chris in three settings to use an appropriate signal to communicate when he was finished with his meal, he began to generalize using the signal in other settings.

Although sequential modification is a useful strategy to promote generalization, it has some limitations. First, the number of settings it will take to produce generalization is not known ahead of time. The teacher must keep targeting the behavior in different settings until generalization is achieved. The number of settings needed to obtain generalization is often different for different students. Even with these limitations, it is an effective strategy to promote the transfer of treatment gains, at least by training other change agents across settings to implement the same intervention program.

Introduce Natural Maintaining Contingencies

This strategy involves systematically introducing the student to specific contingencies in the nontreatment setting in a manner that allows the behavior to be influenced by them (Baer, 1981). As previously discussed, a teacher should incorporate natural contingencies as early as possible during the initial intervention phase. If a student becomes "hooked" on artificial reinforcers, this in itself may hinder the student from transferring the gains to other settings. Because those reinforcers are not likely to occur in the other settings, the student will never be reinforced in the same manner. Without reinforcement, the student is not likely to show the gains made in the treatment settings. Initiating a program with contingencies that are likely to be present in the natural environments helps promote generalization.

Other teachers have promoted generalization by teaching the students to come in contact with naturally occurring reinforcers in the natural environments. For instance, Mr. Barns taught a young boy with developmental disabilities to purchase food in fast food restaurants. The student, named Larry, was 9 years old, and was severely delayed in speech and social development. His speech consisted of approximations of words such as "cu" for "cup." He rarely initiated interactions with others and often exhibited some subtle self-stimulatory behaviors. Larry had a history of tantrumming and being very noncompliant in restaurants. The only time he was quiet was when he was eating his food. The goal of the program was to increase appropriate cooperative behaviors and decrease the disruptive behaviors.

Mr. Barns set up a program that involved partial participation and introducing Larry to the natural positive reinforcers in a restaurant. On each visit, Mr. Barns had Larry initiate some appropriate behavior that would ultimately get Larry the food. For example, Larry would go to the counter and ask for a coke. Even though Larry had limited speech, he was very successful in getting his point across. He would go to the counter and ask for a "co." The woman behind the counter would say, "You want a coke?" Larry would say, "yea." After the woman gave Larry the coke, she would ask him for the money in his hand. Because Larry had no previous experience with money, Mr. Barns gently prompted Larry to give the money to her. After making his first purchase, Larry walked back to the table with a beaming smile on his face. There was no need to provide him with an artificial reinforcer, he was carrying his well-earned reinforcer. Of course, Mr. Barns praised Larry for a job well done. Mr. Barns reported that Larry appeared to have been very happy because he was successful in purchasing his own drink in a fairly independent manner.

Natural contingencies can be very powerful in helping a student learn and to generalize treatment gains made in the classroom. In the above example, the teacher incorporated the principle of partial participation to increase the likelihood that the student would meet success. Meeting success allowed Larry to receive reinforcers as a result of his own efforts. As in Larry's case, students who meet success and receive natural reinforcement become very motivated to remain on-task.

Train Sufficient Exemplars

This approach entails using a sufficient number of exemplars while teaching a student a new concept (Baer, 1981). Years ago, teachers frequently made the error of using only one set of task materials while teaching students common discriminations. After teaching a student one example of a concept, they frequently noted that the student did not generalize the concept to other examples.

For example, I once observed a teacher who spent considerable time teaching a 9-year-old girl with autism to get a plate versus a cup. Unfortunately, when new plates and cups were introduced, the student did not generalize the concepts of plates and cups. During the next few weeks, the teacher proceeded to incorporate a wide variety of different plates and cups which varied in color, size, and material. Eventually, the teacher found that the girl could generalize the concepts of plate and cup with novel sets.

Today, most teachers I work with in special and regular education incorporate multiple exemplars while teaching students a wide variety of concepts. One critical question that needs to be addressed before using this strategy pertains to deciding which exemplars should be used. If a teacher does not pick "good" exemplars, generalization may not occur.

Horner and his colleagues (Horner, Sprague, & Wilcox, 1982), have conducted a systematic line of research focused on developing guidelines for teachers to use when choosing examples of a concept. Referred to as the General Case Analysis approach, Dr. Horner and his colleagues suggest that great care must be taken in choosing the exemplars. The exemplars should represent the wide range of possibilities that may occur in the student's natural environments. Before incorporating specific examples during a lesson to teach a concept or a skill, the teacher should be concerned with how representative the examples are of all those possible in other settings. Using representative examples helps to ensure that a student is truly taught the general case of a concept or new skill and will be more likely to transfer the behavior to other settings.

22

Concluding Comments

> *If we are individualizing our approaches, the number of different successful programs that can be used equals the number of students who need them.*

As has been described in this book, certain principles form the basis of most, if not all, effective intervention programs. Knowing these principles of effective behavioral programming allow teachers to formulate, implement, and evaluate individualized intervention programs. Understanding the principles will help prepare a teacher to deal successfully with new and challenging behaviors and students.

Although the intent of this book is to help prepare teachers, any book has its limitations. In particular, a book cannot provide teachers (or readers) with feedback on their use of the principles as they begin to apply them in their classrooms. Applying the principles and receiving feedback from a trained professional is preferred. After a teacher has applied these principles with several students and received feedback, the teacher eventually can apply them independently to solve new problems.

The examples presented in this book, hopefully, have helped readers learn the basic principles. They were chosen to represent a fairly wide group of students and teachers to stress the idea that most of these principles have implications for all students. After working with many teachers and other professionals, I have seen the utility of these principles. Using them, teachers have promoted the acquisition of very complex and advanced skills by students who otherwise would have had severe difficulties learning. Teachers also have helped students to keep their Least Restrictive Placement by eliminating behavior problems. Perhaps, most importantly, from a teacher's perspective, the correct use of these principles facilitates success not only for students, but for teachers as well.

References

Alberto, P. A., & Troutman, A. C. (1990). *Applied behavior analysis for teachers* (3rd ed.). New York: Macmillan.

Anderson-Inman, L., Paine, S. C., & Deutchman, L. (1984). Neatness counts: Effects of direct instruction and self-monitoring on the transfer of neat-paper skills to nontraining settings. *Analysis and Intervention in Developmental Disabilities, 4,* 137–156.

Azrin, N. H., & Holz, W. C. (1966). Punishment. In W. K. Honig (Ed.), *Operant behavior: Areas of research and application.* New York: Appleton-Century-Crofts.

Baer, D. M. (1981). *How to plan for generalization.* Austin, TX: PRO-ED.

Baer, D. M., Wolf, M. M., & Risley, T. (1968). Current dimensions of applied behavior analysis. *Journal of Applied Behavior Analysis, 1,* 91–97.

Bailey, S. (1983). Extraneous aversives. In S. Axelrod & J. Apsche (Eds.), *The effects of punishment on human behavior* (pp. 247–284). New York: Academic Press.

Barlow, D., & Hayes, S. (1979). Alternating treatments design: One strategy for comparing the effects of two treatments in a single subject. *Journal of Applied Behavior Analysis, 12,* 199–210.

Barlow, D., & Hersen, M. (1984). *Single case experimental designs: Strategies for studying behavior change* (2nd ed.). New York: Pergamon Press.

Becker, W. C., Engelmann, S., & Thomas, D. R. (1975a). *Teaching 1: Classroom management.* Chicago: Science Research Associates.

Becker, W. C., Engelmann, S., & Thomas, D. R. (1975b). *Teaching 2: Cognitive learning and instruction.* Chicago: Teaching Research Associates.

Bellamy, G. T., Horner, R. H., & Inman, D. P. (1979). *Vocational habilitation of severely retarded adults.* Austin, TX: PRO-ED.

Bijou, S. W., Peterson, R. F., & Ault, M. H. (1968). A method to integrate descriptive and experimental field studies at the level of data and empirical concepts. *Journal of Applied Behavior Analysis, 1,* 175–191.

Birnbrauer, J. S., Bijou, S. W., Wolf, M. M., & Kidder, J. D. (1965). Programmed instruction in the classroom. In L. P. Ullmann & L. Krasner (Eds.), *Case studies in behavior modification.* New York: Holt, Rinehart & Winston.

Bloom, L., & Lahey, M. (1978). *Language development and language disorders.* New York: John Wiley.

Catania, A. C. (1984). *Learning* (2nd ed.). Englewood Cliffs, NJ: Prentice-Hall.

Carr, E. G. (1988). Functional equivalence as a mechanism of response generalization. In R. H. Horner, G. Dunlap, & R. L. Koegel (Eds.), *Generalization and maintenance: Life-style changes in applied settings.* Baltimore: Paul H. Brookes.

Carr, E. G., & Durand, V. M. (1985). Reducing behavior problems through functional communication training. *Journal of Applied Behavior Analysis, 18,* 111–126.

Carr, E. G., Newsome, C. D., & Binkoff, J. A. (1980). Escape as a factor in the aggressive behavior in two retarded children. *Journal of Applied Behavior Analysis, 13,* 101–117.

Churchill, D. W. (1971). Effects of success and failure in psychotic children. *Archives of General Psychology, 25,* 208–214.

Cooper, J. O., Heron, T. E., & Heward, W. L. (1987). *Applied behavior analysis.* Columbus, OH: Charles E. Merrill.

Dewson, M., & Whiteley, J. (1987). Sensory reinforcement of head turning with nonambulatory, profoundly mentally retarded persons. *Research in Developmental Disabilities, 8,* 413–426.

Dunlap, G. (1984). The influence of task variation and maintenance tasks on the learning and affect of autistic children. *Journal of Experimental Child Psychology, 37,* 41–64.

Dunlap, G., Koegel, R. L., Johnson, J., & O'Neill, R. (1987). Maintaining performance of autistic clients in community settings with delayed contingencies. *Journal of Applied Behavior Analysis, 20,* 185–191.

Favell, J. E., & Reid, D. H. (1988). Generalizing and maintaining improvements in problem behavior. In R. H. Horner, G. Dunlap, & R. L. Koegel (Eds.), *Generalization and maintenance: Life-style changes in applied settings.* Baltimore: Paul H. Brookes.

Foxx, R. M. (1982). *Decreasing behaviors of severely retarded and autistic persons.* Champaign, IL: Research Press.

Foxx, R. M., & Bechtel, D. R. (1983). Overcorrection: A review and analysis. In S. Axelrod & J. Apsche (Eds.), *The effects of punishment on human behavior* (pp. 133–220). New York: Academic Press.

Gast, D. L., & Nelson, C. M. (1977a). Legal and ethical considerations for the use of timeout in special education settings. *Journal of Special Education, 11,* 457–467.

Gast, D. L., & Nelson, C. M. (1977b). Timeout in the classroom: Implications for special education. *Exceptional Children, 43,* 461–464.

Green, C., Reid, D., White, L., Halford, R., Brittain, D., & Gardner, S. (1988). Identifying reinforcers for persons with profound handicaps: Staff opinion vs. systematic assessment of preferences. *Journal of Applied Behavior Analysis, 21,* 31–43.

Fehr, M., Wacker, D., Trezise, J., Lennon, R., & Meyerson, L. (1979). Visual, auditory, and vibratory stimulation as reinforcers for profoundly retarded children. *Rehabilitation Psychology, 26,* 201–209.

Hall, R. V., & Hall, M. C. (1980). *How to select reinforcers.* Lawrence, KS: H & H Enterprises.

Hartmann, D. P., & Hall, R. V. (1976). The changing criterion design. *Journal of Applied Behavior Analysis, 9,* 527–532.

Hawkins, R. P., & Fabry, B. D. (1979). Applied behavior analysis and interobserver reliability: A commentary on two articles by Birkimer and Brown. *Journal of Applied Behavior Analysis, 12,* 545–552.

Homme, L., Csanyi, A. P., Gonzales, M. A., & Rechs, J. R. (1970). *How to use contingency contracting in the classroom.* Champaign, IL: Research Press.

Horner, R. D., & Baer, D. M. (1978). Multiple-probe technique: A variation of the multiple baseline. *Journal of Applied Behavior Analysis, 11,* 189–196.

Horner, R. H., & Budd, C. M. (1985). Teaching manual sign language to a nonverbal student: Generalization of sign use and collateral reduction of maladaptive behavior. *Education and Training of the Mentally Retarded, 20* (1), 39–47.

Horner, R. H., Dunlap, G., & Koegel, R. L. (Eds.). (1988). *Generalization and maintenance: Life-style changes in applied settings.* Baltimore: Paul H. Brookes.

Horner, R. H., Sprague, J., & Wilcox, B. (1982). Constructing general case programs for community activities. In B. Wilcox & G. T. Bellamy (Eds.), *Design of high school programs for severely handicapped students* (pp. 61–98). Baltimore: Paul H. Brookes.

Iwata, B. A., Dorsey, M. F., Slifer, K. J., Bauman, K. E., & Richman, G. S. (1982). Toward a functional analysis of self-injury. *Analysis and Intervention in Developmental Disabilities, 2,* 3–20.

Kazdin, A. E. (1975). *Behavior modification in applied settings.* Homewood, IL: Dorsey Press.

Kazdin, A. E. (1977). *The token ecomony: A review and evaluation.* New York: Plenum Press.

Kazdin, A. E. (1978). *History of behavior modification.* Baltimore: University Park Press.

Kazdin, A. E., & Bootzin, R. R. (1972). The token economy: An evaluative review. *Journal of Applied Behavior Analysis, 5,* 343–372.

Koegel, R. L., & Egel, A. L. (1979). Motivating autistic children. *Journal of Abnormal Psychology, 88,* 418–426.

Koegel, R. L., Kern Koegel, L., & Schreibman, L. (1991). Assessing and training parents in teaching pivotal behaviors. In R. J. Prinz (Ed.), *Advances in behavioral assessment of children and families* (5th ed., pp. 65–82). London: Jessica Kingsley, Ltd.

Koegel, R. L., O'Dell, M. C., & Koegel, L. K. (1987). A natural language teaching paradigm for nonverbal autistic children. *Journal of Autism and Developmental Disorders, 17,* 187–200.

Koegel, R. L., Russo, D. C., & Rincover, A. (1977). Assessing and training teachers in the generalized use of behavior modification with autistic children. *Journal of Applied Behavior Analysis, 10,* 197–205.

LaNunziata, L. J., Hunt, K. P., & Cooper, J. O. (1984). Suggestions for phasing out token economy systems in primary and intermediate grades. *Techniques, 1,* 151–156.

Lovaas, O. I., & Simmons, J. Q. (1969). Manipulation of self-destruction in three retarded children. *Journal of Applied Behavior Analysis, 2,* 131–166.

Macmillan, D. L. (1971). The problem of motivation in the education of the mentally retarded. *Exceptional Children, 37,* 579–586.

Nelson, C. M., & Rutherford, R. B. (1983). Timeout revisited: Guidelines for its use in special education. *Exceptional Education Quarterly, 3,* 56–67.

O'Leary, S. G., & O'Leary, K. D. (1977). *Classroom management* (2nd ed.). New York: Pergamon Press.

Pace, G., Ivancic, M., Edwards, G., Iwata, B., Page, T. (1985). Assessment of stimulus preference and reinforcer value with profoundly retarded individuals. *Journal of Applied Behavior Analysis, 18,* 249–255.

Parrish, J. M., Cataldo, M. F., Kolko, D. J., Neef, N. A., & Egel, A. L. (1986). Experimental analysis of response covariation among compliant and inappropriate behaviors. *Journal of Applied Behavior Analysis, 19,* 241–254.

Rosenberg, M., & Burke, J. C. (1992). *Social skills assessment and training with behaviorally disordered students.* A presentation for the Baltimore City Schools.

Skinner, B. F. (1969). *Contingencies of reinforcement: A theoretical analysis.* New York: Appleton-Century-Crofts.

Stokes, T. F., & Baer, D. M. (1977). An implicit technology of generalization. *Journal of Applied Behavior Analysis, 10,* 347–367.

Tawney, J., & Gast, D. (1984). *Single-subject research in special education.* Columbus, OH: Charles E. Merrill.

Wilson, P. G., Reid, D. H., Phillips, J. F., & Burgio, L. D. (1984). Normalization of institutional mealtimes for profoundly retarded persons: Effects and noneffects of teaching family-style dining. *Journal of Applied Behavior Analysis, 17,* 189–201.

Winterling, V., Dunlap, G., & O'Neill, R. E. (1987). The influence of task variation on the aberrant behaviors of autistic students. *Education and Treatment of Children, 10,* 105–110.

Glossary

A-B design A single-subject experimental design which has two phases, the baseline phase (A) and a treatment phase (B). Because there is no replication, it may be difficult to demonstrate a cause and effect relationship using this design.

abscissa The horizontal axis on an X-Y graph. This axis is used to represent a time dimension such as days or sessions.

antecedent stimuli Events or stimuli that precede a behavior.

an aversive An event or item delivered contingent on the display of a disruptive behavior which decreases the future likelihood of that behavior occurring. Something the student actively tries to avoid.

back-up reinforcer A highly desired object or event that a student can exchange for a specific number of tokens or points.

baseline A phase in which data are gathered on a person's display of a behavior, prior to the introduction of the intervention program.

baseline data Data collected prior to introduction of an intervention which are compared to data collected during intervention to assess the effects of the program.

behavior An observable and measurable act performed by a person.

behavioral contract Also called a student-teacher contract. Forming a commitment between a student and teacher by specifying the task and the reinforcer that will be earned after completing the task.

behavioral objective A statement that communicates to others a proposed change in a behavior and includes information on who will perform the behavior, what the behavior is, and the degree that the behavior will be changed.

chaining A teaching procedure that involves breaking a complex task down into subcomponents and teaching one component to mastery before adding the other components in a sequential manner.

consequence An event or item that follows the occurrence of a behavior.

contingency The relationship between a target behavior and the consequence that follows, whether it is a punisher or a reinforcer.

deprivation A condition in which an individual has been without a particular reinforcer for a period of time and, therefore, is likely to want to work for it.

duration recording A data collection system used to record the amount of time a behavior lasts.

event recording A data collection system used to record each occurrence of a target behavior.

extinction Withholding reinforcement for a previously reinforced behavior to decrease the likelihood of the behavior occurring again.

fading The gradual removal of a prompt or an entire program.

generalized conditioned punisher Any conditioned punisher that is associated with many other punishers.

generalized conditioned reinforcer A reinforcer that is associated with either a variety of other behaviors or a variety of other reinforcers, which may include primary and backup reinforcers.

group designs A research methodology that involves analyzing data on groups of individuals rather than specific participants.

interval recording A direct observation data recording method that divides a time period into equal units in which an observer records whether the target behavior occurs.

nonseclusionary time-out A version of time-out in which the student is not removed from the situation but entails having the student either partially removed or having the teacher remove the task materials for a brief period of time.

observational data recording system A general strategy of recording data while the student is exhibiting the behavior.

ordinate The vertical axis of an X-Y graph. The axis usually depicts quantity such as percent or number of occurrences.

outcome recording A general strategy used to assess the occurrence of a behavior by having the student produce a permanent product such as a report.

overcorrection A procedure that requires the student to fix the environment caused by his or her disruptive actions plus an additional (reasonable) amount.

positive reinforcement The procedure of presenting a reinforcer contingent on a person's display of a target behavior and that increases the likelihood of that behavior occurring in the future.

primary reinforcer A reinforcer that has a biological importance to an individual such as food or drink.

prompt An added stimulus that is used to facilitate the student's performance of the target response and that is faded over time.

punisher Any event or item that follows an inappropriate behavior in a contingent manner and decreases the likelihood that the behavior will be exhibited in the future.

reinforcer A consequent event or item that is delivered contingent on the display of a behavior and increases the likelihood of that behavior.

reinforcer sampling An informal or formal method of allowing students to sample potential items or events that may serve as reinforcers during an intervention program.

reliability The extent to which two independent observers agree on their observations, usually expressed as a percentage such as agreements divided by agreements plus disagreements multipled by 100.

response-cost A procedure that involves removing a specific amount of a tangible reinforcer, such as tokens, contingent on the student's display of a disruptive behavior.

satiation The state in which a student is full or tired of a particular reinforcer; the opposite of deprivation.

shaping Teaching new behaviors by reinforcing closer and closer approximations of the ideal response.

social reinforcer Positive praise, smiles, attention, or similar responses that a student likes, which are delivered contingent on a positive behavior and will increase the likelihood of that behavior occurring in the future.

time-in A situation that involves allowing the student to have the opportunity to earn positive reinforcement contingent on appropriate, productive classroom behaviors.

time-out A procedure that involves removing the student from all reinforcement for a brief period of time contingent on an inappropriate behavior.

time sampling A direct observation data recording method used to record whether a behavior, or part of a behavior, occurs in a series of discontinuous intervals.

Index

A

A-B-C data, 8–14, 88, 123–126
Antecedent stimuli, 8, 40–46
Applied Behavior Analysis, 7–14, 123–126
Assessing program effectiveness, 147–164

B

Baseline assessment, 148–151
Basic behavioral teaching procedures, 43–59
  chaining, 54–56
  clear instructions and requests, 44–46
  consequences, 60–84
  partial participation, 57–59
  prompts and prompt fading, 46–54
  shaping, 56–57
Behavior problems
  prioritizing, 35–38
  types of
    aggression, 13, 18–19
    disruptions, 8–9
    noncompliance, 19–20, 87–94
    self-injury, 13

Behavior problems, types of *(continued)*
    tantrums, 19
Behavioral contracts, 101–105
Behavioral definitions, 18–20
Behavioral objectives, 169–174

C

Catching them being cooperative and good, 90–93
Classroom contingencies
  specifying the consequences, 89–90, 97–99, 102–105
Counting behaviors and measuring strategies, 20–28
  factors to consider, 29–30
  types of
    automatic recording systems, 21–22
    observational recording systems, 22–28
    permanent products and outcome measurement, 22
Communication skills
  and disruptive behaviors, 115
  methods to promote communication skills, 116–119
Cooperation, 87–94

193

D

Data collection, 8–14
Deprivation of reinforcers, 76
Defining behavior problems, 17–20
Determining functions of disruptive behaviors, 7–14

E

Effective teaching, 4
Extinction, 127

F

Fading
   behavior management programs, 93–94, 99–100, 112–113
   prompts, 49–54
Fixing the environment, 141–143

G

Generalization
   definition of, 174–175
   promotion of
      introducing natural maintaining contingencies, 177–178
      sequential modification, 176–177
      training sufficient exemplars, 178–179
General case analysis approach, 179
Generalized conditioned reinforcers, 67
Graphing, 149–154
Group designs, 147

I

Individualized Education Program
   assessing and programming for generalization, 174–179
   and behavior management programming, 166–179
   behavioral objectives, 169–174
   designing individualized programs, 168–169
Increasing other behaviors that serve the same function, 123–126

M

Motivation, methods to increase, 118–119
Multiple exemplars, 116–117

N

Natural and direct reinforcers, 65–67
Natural maintaining contingencies and generalization, 177–178
Nonseclusionary time-out, 133–134

O

Observer bias, 30
Overcorrection, 141

P

Parent involvement, 38
Planned ignoring, 127–129

Positive classroom behaviors
  defining, 20, 108
  delineating, 37
  methods of increasing, 85–105
Positive practice, 142
Positive reinforcement
  choosing reinforcers, 73–76
  definition of, 63–64
  delivering, 67–72
  fading to naturally occurring reinforcers, 72–73
  types of reinforcers, 64–67, 111–112
Primary reinforcers, 64–65
Program assessment strategies
  A-B comparison, 153–154
  A-B-A-B designs, 160–163
  alternating treatment design, 163–164
  changing criteria design, 163
  multiple-baseline design, 155–160
Punishment
  defining a punisher, 80
  ethical considerations, 79–80, 83–84, 132
  procedural considerations in using, 81–84, 121–122, 135, 138–139

R

Reinforcer sampling, 73–76
Reinforcer stores, 73–74
Reliability
  calculating, 31–32
  problems of, 30–32

Response-cost, 137–139
  and token economy systems, 98–99
Rules, specifying in classroom, 89, 96–97, 101–103, 141–142

S

Satiation, 76, 69–70
Seclusionary time-out, 132–133
Self-monitoring programs, 107–114
  defining behavior, 108–110
  methods of, 113–114
Sensory reinforcement, 64–65
Sequential modification, and generalization, 176–177
Shared control, 43
Single-case experimental designs, 148–164
Social skills, 167–168

T

Task variation, 42–43, 117–118
Teacher-student contracts, 101–105
Time-in setting, 131–132
Time-out procedures, 131–135
Training sufficient exemplars, and generalization, 178–179
Token economy programs, 95–100
  back-up reinforcers, 97–98
  choosing tokens, 96
  listing positive behaviors, 96–97